Table of Contents

Foreword	pg. 2
Introduction	pg. 4
Chapter 1: Identifying Qualified Candidates	pg. 11
Chapter 2: Do Your Homework	pg. 27
Chapter 3: On the Spot	pg. 37
Chapter 4: The Legal Perspective	pg. 52
Chapter 5: Evaluate for Success	pg. 65
Chapter 6: Negotiations: The Art of the Deal	pg. 77
Chapter 7: Onboarding: Accommodate, Acclimate, and Accelerate New Members to the Team	pg. 87
Chapter 8: Retention: Keep Your Best at Their Best	pg. 101
Chapter 9: Regrouping: When Good Decisions Go Bad	pg. 117
Chapter 10: When is it time to call a recruiter?	pg. 124
Conclusion	pg. 132
Acknowledgements	pg. 137
About the author	pg. 141

Foreword

So, I get this call from Henry asking me to write a foreword for this book that you have before you. I have known Henry Glickel, CERS, for many years now. I think we met at a New England Conference some 15 plus years ago. I honestly cannot remember, not that it matters. I immediately say, "...of course, I would be delighted." I hang up the phone after a couple of minutes of conversation and ask myself, "Okay, now what?"

As President of the National Association of Personnel Services (NAPS) and affiliated with this organization since 1982, I know I can do this, how hard can it be? I have been in the recruiting and staffing industry for over 35 years. While I consider myself experienced and older, I don't feel so old because I really love this business. In fact, during my tenure with the National Association of Personnel Services, I actually coined their tag line that later became the web site name: "Recruitinglife.com; because, it's more than a job, it's your life! The fact of the matter is – if you take this profession seriously – it is so much more than a job, it IS your life. Those that are dedicated, truly live and breathe this business, and it does become their life.

Henry Glickel, CERS, (Certified Employee Retention Specialist) is one who lives and breathes this business. Henry is like that proverbial kid in the candy shop when he talks about what he does. Henry is correct when he explains that so many people don't realize that what we do is actually fantastic. Think about it. What Henry and those of us in this profession are doing is finding people a job, a career! Finding a person a job (in our world, we call that a placement, making a placement, placing a person) is akin to scoring the winning goal in a soccer match (been there, done that, in a previous life!) or coming up on stage for that extra curtain call. It's just a great "warm and fuzzy feeling." You get to do this over and over again, often many times a month.

My job here is that of an emcee. I am introducing you to Henry and to this book. To do my job correctly, one must actually read the book – which I have. In discussions about the book with Henry, he equates this book to a cookbook. I actually liked his analogy, but I believe it is much more than a listing of the ingredients and how to prepare the meal (the hiring of a candidate).

This book is a map though that jungle of a world out there we call hiring, with some recipes for some great snacks along the way. Not only will you be able to find your way through the maze, but you will be satisfied when you're at your journey's end.

Henry takes you thru that process, step by step, and shows you the way with solid examples and illustrations, making each chapter very clear in terms of what must be done, the order in which it should be done and even consequences when we don't follow the road map (or the recipe for that snack along the way).

Finally, I asked Henry why he wrote this book. Yes, Henry Glickel, CERS, most definitely lives and breathes this profession. For all I know, he even bleeds the color of this profession! Henry wants all who read this book to know what's involved, how he reads the map to get you out of the hiring maze and prepares the recipes for success in his profession. In fact, he makes it look rather easy. But making it look easy doesn't mean that it is! I believe that there will always be a need for great recruiters. We all have our jobs that must be done, and I also believe that you should leave specific jobs to specific experts. Henry Glickel, CERS, is an expert.

John Sacerdote, President
National Association of Personnel Services

Introduction

Recruiting is such a neat business. We get to see people at their best and we get to see people at their worst. We get to reach out to them sometimes when they least expect to hear from us, and we can see their true colors.

I've conducted, literally, thousands of searches in my career and there is one clear-cut, predominant theme: People are looking for potential, whether it's potential in a position, a career, a company, a supervisor. Whatever the case may be, people are looking beyond the obvious toward the promise of possibility.

As a hiring manager, so are you.

As an individual, you appreciate the value of finding the right fit for something that's important to you. If you're going to make an investment, you want to be certain you're making a wise decision and have sufficiently explored the possibilities and evaluated your options. You don't want to settle.

You devote hours to finding the perfect house. You compare and test drive to find the perfect car. You research to find the best computer. You shop around and try on to find the perfect suit.

Finding that perfect fit of a person for your open position is even more overwhelming. You can't test drive or try on a job candidate. There's just so much to consider, so much to evaluate, references that must be checked, investment in training and onboarding. There's a great deal of time and thought involved and you're often in a hurry to fill a vacant position and get back to business.

Compounding the challenge is the changing face of the labor pool. The U.S. Bureau of Labor Statistics' *Occupational Outlook Handbook, 2012-13 Edition, Overview of the 2010-20 Projections* states that:

- "The primary working-age group, those between 25 and 54 years old, is projected to decline from 66.9 percent of the labor force in 2010 to 63.7 percent in 2020."

- "The share of workers aged 55 years and older is anticipated to go from 19.5 percent to 25.2 percent of the labor force during the same period."

- The shift in the U.S. economy away from goods-producing in favor of service-providing is expected to continue.

- "Employment of sales managers is expected to grow 12 percent from 2010 to 2020, about as fast as the average for all occupations. As the economy grows, organizations will focus on generating new sales through more effective sales management."

- "Like the population, the labor force is growing more slowly, becoming older and more diverse."

- The number of women in the labor force will grow at a slightly faster rate than the number of men.

- "Jobs requiring a master's degree are expected to grow the fastest."

What's more, sales managers and their departments comprise critical personnel in a company and are therefore less subject to outsourcing than other types of managers. In addition, in this era of keen competition, companies are finding many of the best candidates are already satisfactorily employed – they are not looking for your job!

The Aberdeen Group's 2009 Talent Acquisition Report stated that "while hiring may slow or stop, talent acquisition at top-performing companies never does." You should always be looking for those top producers and working to further develop your team, so even if you're not working to fill an immediate vacancy, you need to know what's out there.

Research also showed that, "despite the massive numbers of unemployed workers in the marketplace, the gap between the skills required by businesses and what's available in the talent pool is widening."

According to the Bureau of Labor Statistics, "Sales and related occupations are expected to add 980,400 new jobs by 2018, growing by 6 percent."

But perhaps the harshest reality is that a bad hire can affect your bottom line. I estimate that the cost to replace an employee ranges conservatively from $10,000 and up. Costs associated with turnover are threefold: separation costs, replacement costs and productivity costs. Separation costs can include everything from severance pay, human resource time for exit interviews, outplacement fees and maybe even litigation costs.

Frequently bemoaned replacement costs include numerous sourcing expenses, processing costs associated with screening, interviewing, assessing and evaluating candidates, human resource and management time expended throughout the process, travel and relocation expenses, as well as signing bonuses, and orientation, onboarding and training costs.

Productivity costs may include down time and start-up time, lost sales, lost customers, reduced customer service, and much more. In addition to financial considerations, there may also be administrative, legal and reputation repercussions.

I had a vice president of a company with an interesting children's product line call me years ago to provide recruiting services to his company.

He had about eight inside sales reps and six outside sales reps. The company was riddled with significant turnover.

The company representatives interviewing prospective employees loved to talk about the opportunity for promotion, but the fact was it was a small company with less than 60 employees and there was little room for promotion. The vice president we were working with had been there 18 years, had moved up through attrition and had been in his present position for 12 years, but there they were, telling candidates about the opportunity for promotion.

What they found was that the candidates were people looking for stability and progression making them eager to get the positions, but then reality would set in and they would find that there was nowhere to go, and they would leave. Each sales position was turning over about twice a year!

The company was not considering the three to four months it took to train these people or the $40,000-45,000 salaries and start-up costs, but rather at the assertive, eager personalities they could get three to six months out of and then move on. They were not looking at what they were losing over the long run.

I call it being penny-wise and people-foolish. Too often in an effort to quickly fill a vacant position, hiring managers will cut corners somewhere in the hiring process in the name of efficiency. Or worse, management may not be willing to spend the money to secure the level of talent the position requires. Saving money today will not help you build your team or boost your bottom line for the future.

Where does all this leave you with your crucial, yet vacant position? As more companies vie for a smaller skilled labor pool while also working to meet the long-term needs and goals of their business, several things must come into focus:

- Clearly identify and define the skills, attributes and behaviors most critical in productive employees.

- Successfully evaluate to find the strongest possible candidates.

- Negotiate with an attractive, competitive offer.

- Effectively onboard to welcome, acclimate and facilitate success.

- Effective retention efforts to motivate, engage and encourage your work force and ultimately demonstrate that your organization is a great place to work.

- Frank evaluation of all processes and corporate culture to see where improvements can be made.

In addition to managing your business you must also be in the business of talent management. When it comes to hiring and retention, you must see what others do not. You do it in the business world; why not apply it to your people? See why your most successful people succeed and your less successful do not. See what motivates them. See what keeps them happy and consider that people may only be good in a position for so long. Develop a process to proactively look for your next staff. Upgrade, raising the level of people you have.

This brings to mind yet another challenge facing hiring managers: the human element. There are every manner of variables involved when dealing with individual human beings. Each has their own set of emotions, motivations, drives, aspirations, grievances, likes and dislikes, circumstances, obstacles, and etcetera. Personal, psychological and emotional factors are involved throughout the entire search, hiring and onboarding processes and cannot be disregarded.

Recruiters refer to this aspect as human capital, and my colleague Stuart Goldblatt states that "Performance for human capital cannot be predicted. It's the life of a recruiter. You just never know how people will perform, what they will do, or what will happen."

Stu had a sad case that he doesn't like to talk about, but it puts things into perspective. He had a young, 28-year-old candidate who was due to start in a new position the Monday after Thanksgiving. He passed away unexpectedly Sunday night. No one could have predicted that.

It's this unpredictable element of human nature and the human condition that we do our best to navigate. Years of working with people give you some understanding of what to expect, but there's always that little factor of the unknown when it comes right down to it.

While there are a number of practical, tactical and formulaic approaches to the intricate processes involved in hiring your perfect candidate, the human elements cannot be overlooked. Ultimately, these non-quantifiable elements could make all the difference in finding the ideal candidate to fill your position.

Be warned: advice on resume writing and finding your "dream job" is everywhere. People with no recruiting or hiring experience recommend all manner of job hunting without any practical knowledge of the process. Unfortunately, some of the best candidates may be engaging in bad advice from many of these sources and some of the worst candidates are engaging in unconventional behavior to get your attention. All of this can put the hiring manager's time at risk and cloud an already murky view of the labor pool. Be cautious!

Success today means that you must develop new methods in sourcing, securing and retaining the best people you can afford. In the case of small businesses, you must make it your competitive mission to be more nimble, flexible and focused on outmaneuvering the larger competition.

All companies must first clearly define the need and the elements involved in the success to meet that need. You then must move to action knowing what questions to ask in the process, which actionable items are necessary, and evaluating with a decisive focus on the end result.

Finding and retaining top quality people is imperative for your business. Hiring is indeed a mission critical to the core success of your business. The task of finding, attracting and retaining that perfect hire is unquestionably daunting.

This book is designed to walk you through these key efforts.

Chapter 1:

Identifying qualified candidates

"The easiest job in the world has to be coroner. Surgery on dead people. What's the worst thing that could happen? If everything went wrong, maybe you'd get a pulse." – Dennis Miller

The open position you're looking to fill is not an easy position. You can't afford to put just any body in there and hope for the best. It's a critical role involved in the intricate system of your company that helps move you toward your corporate goals.

Neither is the task of filling the vacancy easy. You know from experience that success takes time, attention to detail and persistent dedication. But your time is divided between finding the right candidate and running your business. You need things to progress quickly and smoothly, allowing you to stay focused.

On the one hand, the present economy has given rise to many eager and otherwise hard-working but unemployed people looking for a job. Some may be looking to make a change, having settled for a lesser prospect in order to maintain income and retain benefits. On the other hand, the most qualified people are not always available to read your ad. Why? They are already hard at work for someone else, making calls, delivering client presentations, completing sales -- not even looking for your opportunity to come their way.

Generally, when you envision your ideal candidate, you're thinking about the "A" players, the top 25% of the working world who are successful, accomplished and self-motivated. Usually these people are not out there looking for your job so you need to be creative in your efforts to reach them.

The "B" players are often unhappy with their present company and not strongly connected. These candidates may have capabilities that need the right motivation and development.

The great players are decisive problem solvers. They're resilient self-starters willing to help others and the team. They offer valuable experience and skills. Consider your corporate culture and how you encourage the great players and whether or not you can develop the B players.

Take an objective look at your company and consider your accessible resources, the time available to cultivate the right people, and the commitment your company is willing to make to the process. Then go to the drawing board.

In the very beginning stages your search is a blank slate. There is untapped potential just waiting for you to make the most of it.

I was fortunate to work with an office equipment company once that gave us a blank slate. We were able to start from the ground up and develop a recruiting budget and process that helped address timing and defining, important elements for this company at this particular time. We were able to identify very specific processes, timing and other factors that helped move the process along and define the company, resulting in lowered costs and reduced turnover.

Take the time and be objective. Really consider who your company is, what your company wants, and how you're going to get it.

Job Description

When you are recruiting for your company, take the opportunity to make improvements. Commitment to improvement should be a core value of your company anyway. You want to be able to be decisive toward that end, to be able to make choices based on a function of values. The job description is the ideal starting point and is too often taken too lightly.

In the simplest sense, a job description is the official written account of the position to be filled. It describes your needs. It supplies the basics of what the candidate can expect from your company. In addition to being used to advertise the vacant position, the job description may also be used to determine compensation and as a basis for performance reviews.

The job description is also the tool you'll use to attract interest in the position. If it's not accurate and clear, you are not likely to generate suitable interest. Consider the job description a communications tool and take the time to prepare and use it effectively.

Whether you need to fill an existing position or you are creating a new one, the job description can help streamline the candidate identification process and will determine where you go from there. First and foremost, make sure you understand your own needs!

Take some time to evaluate the position and determine whether it should be tweaked to meet any changing needs of the company. Look at what worked when the position was last filled, as well as what didn't work. What did you appreciate about the last employee? What did you wish had been different? Then conduct a job analysis to look at the tasks, sequence of tasks and qualifiers necessary to perform the job.

Many companies are confronted with the challenge of finding employees that demonstrate salesmanship. A company can have a strong product or service, so salesmanship may be less obvious. In a bad economy it can be difficult to gauge whether there is a problem with the product or service or whether the problem lies with salesmanship. During a bad economy it's even more important to be certain you're hiring people with strong salesmanship skills. You'll need a variety of qualifiers to determine this and you'll want to establish these qualifiers from the outset in your job description.

The ideal job description should clearly and concisely communicate your precise needs: what the job entails, responsibilities, reporting structure, expectations and qualifications.

1. Determine 5-10 key responsibilities
2. Delineate expected goals/objectives
3. Outline behavioral characteristics
4. Define reporting structure
5. Indicate 3-5 qualifications
6. Determine basic requirements, skills and credentials

Components:

- Title of the position
- Department
- Overall responsibilies
- Key areas of responsibility
- Term of employment
- Qualifications, including skills and experience required

Additional considerations:

- Travel requirements
- Benefits
- Bonuses

Some caution is required when addressing educational and experience requirements to avoid inadvertent discrimination. Be sure the educational requirements stated are a true necessity for the job. If the job may be accomplished by someone with equivalent experience but not necessarily a specific credential, the job description may need to be re-examined. In addition, to avoid age discrimination, it may be best to list minimum years of experience required without suggesting an upper limit.

Job descriptions can have some legal implications, as they provide a basis for job evaluation, wage and salary comparison and equitable wage and salary structure (under the Equal Pay Act). They may be used to help determine a position's exempt or non-exempt status under the Fair Labor Standards Act, and to provide a basis from which to determine whether an applicant with a disability is qualified for the job, as well as what accommodation is required to perform the essential functions of the job under the Americans with Disabilities Act.

Ads

Attracting great talent is a challenge. Your ad is the first step in the communication process designed to meet that challenge. The goal of your ad is to attract qualified interest, communicate the nature of the position quickly and clearly, and to direct a response process and mechanism. Keep in mind that a large percentage of the candidates you want to attract are already well settled, so your ad needs to be descriptive, but attractive enough to appeal to these otherwise passive candidates.

The ad should follow the classic formula:

- Attention
- Interest
- Desire
- Action

Generally, the headline - usually the job title itself - will attract the immediate attention of the appropriate candidates. Be sure to write out the full title of the position. Do not abbreviate. Be specific so a candidate will look at the job description further and know what to expect.

The first paragraph is critical. It needs to grab the attention of appropriate candidates and spark a call to action. Include your job description. Your ad will gain the interest from those who meet your requirements.

At the same time, you don't want to discourage potentially strong candidates with long lists of requirements that may not be truly essential. Often an ad can list so many requirements as to be restrictive. Perhaps a viable candidate sees the ad but does not meet every requirement and is therefore discouraged from submitting a resume.

Before drafting the ad, consider those aspects that are absolutely required for the position and those that are on your wish list. Is an MBA essential or simply desired? Once you have established a list of definitive requirements, prioritize in order of importance and list them accordingly.

To further engage the reader, use the second person so the appropriate candidates can picture themselves in your position: "You will report to...", "You will be required to..." Generally use language that the reader uses, using bullet points and short paragraphs. Keep it simple.

Create desire by relating the job's appeal and rewards. Briefly relate what makes your company appealing or why it is a good place to work. Let the candidate know what's in it for him. Branding should be present but not overpowering.

The call to action should clearly direct the candidate how and where to submit a resume. Again, keep it simple and easy to follow.

Design of the ad should focus on clarity of text. The layout should convey a professional image and be easy to follow.

Finally, be sure to place your ad where it will likely catch the attention of your target audience. The electronic age has shifted job search efforts to online forums. General listings aggregators such as Career Builder, Monster and Hot Jobs readily come to mind. In addition, more specialized job search engines also are available.

Website

Most corporate websites these days include a career page. Typically these are not very compelling and do not meet with a lot of success in filling open positions.

Keep in mind that top talent will research your company nearly much as you'll research them. Evaluate your website to be sure it clearly projects your corporate image and consistently communicates your mission and vision. To be sure your site is user-friendly, keep it clean and simple. Avoid graphics and animation that take too long to load.

Candidates are likely to view the "About Us" page of your company website as well as any biographies of the management team. Keep these concise, informative and easy to navigate.

Prominently display a link to your career page prominently on the company home page so users will see it and can quickly react. Include an online application option so users can readily apply online and allow them to email or upload their resume. Be sure your site conveys the benefits of working for your company. Let prospective candidates see what's in it for them, what makes your company a good place to work.

You may want to include "reviews" from existing employees. Prospective candidates appreciate hearing how current employees feel about working for the company. Highlight benefits information and available training so candidates can see if you fit in with their short- and long-term goals, and if your company would contribute to their work-life balance. If there is interesting local history at your location, recreational and social opportunities, and other facts they may find relevant, you may want to note these as well.

One company I work with includes stories and backgrounds in the bios of their employees, in addition to their job experience. They've found that candidates who look at these employee bios feel a connection and think, "If he can do it, I could do it." They can relate to certain employees before they even start, allowing the company to define a particular set of characteristics, enabling them to source according to background similarities and perceived values. It's a great tool that the company still uses today, almost 10 years later.

Finally, when working on your website, search engine optimization is critical. Be sure that key words relevant to the demographic of the job seekers you wish to attract are included on your Career page. Do your research. Update every three to four weeks to stimulate search engines and keep things fresh.

Job Boards

Job boards enable a wider audience reach for a longer period of time. The position is posted 24 hours a day, seven days a week for as long as you like.

Research indicates that the average age of people using job sites is about 35. The sites are user-friendly so candidates need not be tech savvy to peruse open positions. What's more, it's just as easy for you, the employer, to post your position. Just have your job description along with your credit card ready.

So what's the catch? There is the potential for "candidate spam," an abundance of inappropriate resumes bombarding you. While some candidate-filtering or screening software may be available to help you sift through the pile of incoming resumes, you could find yourself spending quite a bit of time on the process.

Once on the cutting-edge of job search technology, job boards are slowly going the way of the Sunday Classifieds. Mobile influence, social media and other technology are changing the way people do almost everything – including search for and apply for jobs. Don't rule out the job boards, but be wary and be prepared.

Job aggregators, such as Simply Hired and Indeed, are search engines that consolidate job postings from many sources. Some are free while others offer pay-per-click models and sponsored models to help move up your posting within the listing category. Job aggregators may also provide you with an onslaught of candidates.

Social media

Millions of people are on Facebook, LinkedIn and Twitter. These and other social media sites facilitate networking in a digital age, enabling up-to-the-minute contact with potential candidates. These venues encourage a more personal approach where branding can be better tailored to the appropriate demographic. Social media sites can also be more easily updated than a corporate website with news of open positions, promotions, incentives, etcetera, making them more dynamic.

The key with social media is to find the right balance.

- **Listen.** People tend to discuss things in a very open way in the social media forum. You can learn a lot with a little review.
- **Interact.** If you find a strong candidate, consider making contact through a private message. Express your interest and share a bit about the company or the position.

- **Exercise caution.** Know where to draw the line. In this day and age of once you hit send, it's out there forever. Keep in mind that there is much that is better left for in-person discussion. If the candidate is interested, let him know that further discussion will take place face-to-face.

My advice is to abide by the provisions of Appendix C to Part 601 Notice of Users of Consumer Reports of the Fair Credit Reporting Act (http://www.fdic.gov/regulations/laws/rules/6500-2700.html). Abide by a set of standards for fair treatment of the individual you're looking at and establish clear language in your candidate screening process.

With over one billion users, Facebook is the largest social networking site today. Many companies are finding ways to make use of the Facebook phenomenon and both Facebook and Twitter are becoming critical tools in the hiring process.

In 2012 Facebook launched its own interactive job board that aggregates 1.7 million openings from a number of well-known job boards. The site is a partnership with the U.S. Department of Labor, the National Association of Colleges and Employers, Direct Employers Association and the National Association of State Workforce Agencies. The page enables users to search for jobs by location, industry and skill, apply to them directly through Facebook, and then share the jobs to their social network. While the app initially had some kinks to work out and some users encountered their share of frustrations, Facebook is ever evolving and this app is likely to evolve as well.

Jobs can also be posted on Facebook Marketplace or placed as an advertisement. The ad enables you to target a more specific group of people by asking you a series of questions regarding the characteristics of people you want to see the ad. Facebook calculates how many users fit that criteria, and you can choose to pay-per-click or per-impression and determine whether you want to run the ad continuously or for a certain period of time.

Your company's own Facebook Page, or your public profile, is another tool that enables you to share your business and product information with Facebook users. Your page should be kept current and relevant and is a good place to post your latest job openings. As with every other aspect of your marketing strategy, make sure you have clear goals in mind for your Facebook page and that any job postings are in keeping with those goals.

Some things to keep in mind when maintaining your Facebook page are:

- Post regularly, but don't overdo it.
- Provide content that is valuable to the user.
- "Listen" as much as you "talk."

The LinkedIn website is the most developed online business and career oriented networking site, claiming more than 175 million professionals use LinkedIn to exchange information, ideas and opportunities. LinkedIn enables users to build a professional online network that may include co-workers, clients, business associates, friends and family.

You can post a job for a fee, search candidates and take advantage of numerous resources the site has available. Job postings can also be placed among groups of which you are a member.

If you find a potential candidate on LinkedIn, you can evaluate, on the spot, by reviewing their profile and recommendations. LinkedIn Recruiter, a premium service, allows companies to view and search through every single profile on the network.

Twitter is a social networking and microblogging service that uses instant messaging. With a Twitter account you can tweet jobs that are available. Twitter Job Search allows you to post available positions.

You can also search for talent by keyword, industry, location and more. Hash tags (#) with a keyword enable you to filter and find relevant information quickly and easily and can help your recruiting effort stand out as candidates do the same to search for a desired position.

Twitter allows only 140 characters to convey a message, so be direct: "Looking for a Sales Rep in NYC, very competitive salary, apply at (include a shortened url using Bitly.com)."

Use hash tags to make your job stand out. Including a hash tag with a keyword in your tweet, it becomes instantly searchable. Some examples of useful hash tags: #job, #jobpost, #employment, #recruiting, #hiring, #career, #staffing, #salesjob, #NAJ (that's Twitter lingo for 'Need A Job?'). You can use more than one hash tag in your message, but keep in mind that characters are limited, so you need to be strategic in which hash tag or tags you use.

Some job boards also offer forums where job seekers can ask questions and request feedback from other job seekers. These may provide another opportunity to develop relationships. You may pose your own questions and connect with candidates offline.

While you can use social media to attract candidates, you can also take advantage of the opportunity to review their information on a more personal level. Private lives are rapidly becoming more public. Just as non-tangible traits affect your rapport with a candidate, what they choose to display on their social media pages may influence your opinion.

Some elements you may want to consider when evaluating a candidate on Facebook:

- Does the candidate show regard for the overlap between personal and professional forums?
- Does the candidate take extreme positions on politics, religion, etc. or does he remain non-controversial?
- Is he a member of relevant groups relating to his field?

- Does he update regularly?

Some elements to consider on LinkedIn:

- How complete is the profile?
- Are there genuine recommendations from appropriate sources such as managers, previous employers, colleagues etc.?
- Is the candidate a member of relevant groups relating to his field?
- How large is the candidate's network?

Some elements to consider for Twitter:

- Does the candidate tweet reasonably, between 2-10 times per day?
- Does the candidate have a strong following ratio?
- Does he or she have a good-sized network?
- Does he oe she maintain an equitable balance between personal and professional posts?
- Does he or she respond to others, as well as update?

If your company maintains a corporate blog, you can use it as a means to attract attention to your position and open a dialogue with potential candidates. Again, be sure your blog accurately projects your corporate image and corporate culture, and is updated with relevant information on a regular basis.

An effective blog is:

- **Enlightening**. You want to inform, not sell. A good blog can serve as a testimonial to your company.

- **Compelling**. People are busy. They will only continue to read if you give them a reason to do so. Make sure your content provides value.

- **Timely**. Blogs should be published with some regularity, perhaps once a week. Whatever schedule you decide, maintain it and stay up to date.

Recruiters

If time is of the essence, and it usually is, let an expert handle the process for you. A recruiter can present you with pre-qualified candidates with much of the screening already done for you. Even in an age with a heavy reliance on social networking, the value of personal connections cannot be overlooked.

Often the best candidates are gainfully employed and not necessarily seeking new opportunities. The relationships recruiters have established with this top talent could be extremely helpful in identifying the most qualified candidates for your position.

I've placed some candidates as many as two, three, or four times over the course of their careers. It's great to see these individuals succeed and grow.

I worked with one individual who I placed in a medical position. He did exceptionally well. I later placed him with an international company who was working to gain a presence in the US. When that company went out of business some time later, I was able to place that same candidate again in another medical position.

To this day I can pick up the phone any time and call him because of the relationship that developed through the years. I, as a recruiter, have that connection with him and he may come to mind when a particular client is looking to fill a position.

Having completed more than 1,500 searches in my life and conducted tens of thousands of interviews, it's very rewarding to see the positive impact I, as a recruiter, have had on a candidate's life. I find that if you treat candidates well and are forthright with them, remaining open and honest, you'll place the best candidates because everyone is on the same page. There's a clear understanding of expectations and there is a sense of mutual respect.

Many recruiters offer a range of services, allowing you to choose only the services of interest to you. Determine the amount of time you have to spend throughout the stages of the hiring process and decide which aspects are best left to the recruiter.

Some say sourcing potential candidates is the easiest part of the hiring process. Evaluating, selecting and negotiating can be much more intricate. These areas may actually be where you need to really do your homework.

It's also important to know your limits. You may simply have too many demands on your time to devote the time needed to all aspects of the hiring process, or you may feel that your judgment is clouded by other equally pressing business concerns. Decide when it's in you or your company's best interest to engage a recruiter.

When choosing a recruiter, you may want to ask these questions:

- How long have you been in business?
- What type of clients do you represent?
- Do you have candidates available?
- How do you check qualifications?
- How much do your recruiters collaborate?
- What is the time range for the recruiting process?
- What is your placement success rate?
- Can I choose just the services I want?

- Do you require an exclusivity agreement?
- What do you expect from me?

This may seem like a lot of things to consider just to identify qualified candidates, but it's important to get off to a strong start in your search. It would be great if someone could give you a roadmap directly to those qualified candidates, but few things that are truly worthy are that easy to come by. Take the time to consider the basics and your search should progress smoothly from there.

Chapter 2:

Do Your Homework

Once you've identified potential candidates it's time to prepare for the interview. Even with an entry level position, the time, costs and other resources entailed in the hiring process are great. That investment is even greater when seeking to fill a higher level position.

Why interviews fail

First, let's take a brief look at some common mistakes that could impact the effectiveness of your interview. We'll spend more time on the art of the interview itself in the next chapter, but let's take a moment to see where managers typically go wrong.

Generic questions. Vague questions prompt vague answers. You need to know what you're looking for and what types of questions will provide that insight. At the same time, you can't be afraid to ask the uncomfortable questions you might be apt to steer away from. Probe with more detailed questions in order to get the detailed information you need.

Too much talking – from you! Although you will need to actively guide the candidate through the interview with questions designed to draw out the information you need, make sure you're listening more than talking. You need to hear what the candidate has to say so you can evaluate later.

Gut feelings. You may feel you're good at reading people, and you may well be. But relying too much on intuition can impact your judgment. Subconsciously people tend to be drawn to people who are most like themselves, but it's critical to remain objective.

Lack of preparation. "Winging it" invariably makes you more inclined to fall back on cliché questions that will not get you enough of the information you need to make a smart hiring decision. Preparation is the key to all interviews. Too many times there is not a consensus of expectations from the management team before the hiring process beings.

One client told me about a candidate who had passed three interviews before being scheduled to have the "final" interview with the vice president of sales. When the candidate was asked to describe his understanding of the job, it turned out that his expectations were completely different from those of the vice president. The candidate's expectations had been defined from the three previous interviews with members of the company, and everyone had had a different view.

Your success in hiring a qualified candidate that will suit your organization depends as much on your preparation as on the interview itself. How can you fill your open position as quickly and successfully as possible without compromising the outcome? It is very important to take a systematic approach to this process.

It's also important to keep in mind that good candidates are not necessarily good at interviews; they can't practice interviewing because they're busy doing their job. A good interview is an opportunity for the hiring authority to extract the information necessary to determine the viability of a candidate. If you ask the right questions that elicit thoughtful non-rehearsed remarks, you'll have a better chance of uncovering a better candidate.

Preparation is the key.

Defining the ideal candidate

You've defined the job description. You have some idea of the talent pool you've identified as likely to interview. Now it is critical to gear every aspect of the hiring process toward your vision of the ideal candidate.

Take the time to define the character of the perfect hire. What are the required skills, competencies and behaviors you want to see in your employee? Keeping in mind that every effective employee brings more to the table than a simple set of skills. Consider how the new hire can potentially add strength, flexibility and responsiveness to your team.

Use the job description as the basis for the responsibilities and skill sets required for the position. List the skills, training, experience, knowledge base, talents and abilities associated with the requirements indicated in the job description. Consider the values, characteristics, personality and professional habits or behaviors that further reflect your ideal candidate. Take into account both attributes, as well as behaviors such as strong communication skills and agreeable manner of speaking. Consider what can be learned and what can't be learned. Think about what will motivate and drive your ideal candidate.

Pre-hire assessment of your specific needs and the competencies required for the job will help you establish an "ideal candidate profile." If you are filling an existing position, consider how previous employees have performed in the job. Identify the success factors and note any areas that were in need of improvement. What were the strengths and weaknesses involved in the role before?

Determine expectations: what do you expect the person in the position to accomplish? By creating a "wish list" of what constitutes your ideal candidate, you will be better able to hire someone who most closely meets your "perfect employee" picture. Many intangibles come into play when defining your ideal candidate.

The following are some attributes to consider when creating your ideal employee wish list:

- Leadership
- Client Service
- Proactive or Reactive
- Follow-Up
- Communication
- Organization
- People skills
- Project Management
- Sense of urgency
- Attention to detail
- Positive Attitude
- Teamwork

Keep in mind the need to be realistic. Creating your ideal candidate profile is not about turning "nice-to-have" characteristics into "must-haves." It's using your experience with top performers to determine a systematic, thorough list of attributes you know will enable a qualified candidate to succeed in your position. I recommend four to six discernible characteristics that top performers in a particular job have in common.

Phone interview

It may be most efficient to conduct an initial interview over the phone. This is a good screening opportunity and makes it easier to cut the interview short should you quickly determine the person to be a non-viable candidate.

You can get a feel for how the candidate will fit into your organization with some simple questions during a phone interview such as:

- What makes our position attractive to you at this time?
- Why are you looking to leave your present position?
- What type of work environment are you looking for?
- What type of compensation package are you seeking?
- Will you travel?
- Will you relocate?
- What are your career goals?
- What are your greatest strengths?
- What was your greatest accomplishment?

I usually recommend keeping phone interviews to just 10-15 minutes to screen some of the top candidates who look appealing on paper. First and foremost, you get a good idea of their phone presence. You can get a sense of how the individual adjusts to the unexpected phone call and how they think on their feet in an unplanned conversation.

Introduce yourself, explain why you are calling and ask if it's a good time to talk. Since you are likely calling at their present job, they may need to schedule a phone interview at a later time.

Some things to consider during the phone interview: does the candidate sound confident? Do you have to repeat yourself? If you were a customer, would you want to speak to him/would you continue speaking with him? How good is his vocabulary? How focused is he? When he talks about what he wants, is he energetic, enthusiastic, does he have conviction about what he is looking for?

Phone interviews can save time in the long run by helping to screen candidates. You can gain valuable insight and gauge interest to see if it's worthwhile to bring the candidate in for further discussion.

Prepare for the interview

The goal of the face-to-face interviewing process is to answer some basic questions:

- Can the candidate do the job and do it well?
- Is he motivated and interested in the position?
- Will he fit into our corporate culture?

Once you have determined who you're going to interview in person, it is best to have a well-defined interview process clearly in place. Set aside the appropriate amount of time for your top candidates. Decide which other members of your team you'd like to meet with the candidate. You will have a more complete and balanced perspective if several people within your organization meet the candidate. In addition to the human resource representative and reporting manager, you may want to add one or two people with whom the candidate would be working.

Let the candidate know what to expect from the interview: How many people he will meet with and how much time he will spend at your company. Read the resume to be sure you have a good understanding of the candidate's experience, but use it as a guide for the interview rather than a complete roadmap.

Consider the location of the interview. The location is a reflection of the company. Select one that is quiet, neat and professional.

While many interviewers tend to assess a candidate on a more emotional level in the first few minutes of meeting, you want to go beyond your "gut instinct" and have a more quantifiable means of evaluating each candidate. Take the time to organize and be prepared.

To ensure that your interview remains focused, prepare a list of questions centered on the key competencies you've defined for your ideal candidate. You will want to use a variety of techniques to learn as much as possible, including open-ended questions, behavioral questions, and periods of silence to gauge the candidate's responses to each. Interview questions fall into several main categories.

Traditional questions elicit general information about a candidate's skills and experience. These are asked so often that candidates are generally prepared for them, so asking these in the early stage of the interview may help the candidate feel more at ease. Examples include:

- What are your greatest strengths?
- What is your experience?
- Why do you want to work for us?

Behavioral questions lead candidates to think on their feet and relate stories as to how they've addressed past job-related challenges and opportunities. If a person has continually achieved success in the past, that behavior is likely to continue.

In addition to learning about the candidate's abilities, as he tells his stories you will discover his communication skills, level of enthusiasm, method of presentation, strategizing to meet his goals, etc. Behavior questions also help provide some indication of how the candidate will fit into your corporate culture. Be prepared to steer the interview, but expect to listen more than talk as the candidate provides his answers.

Some examples of behavioral questions include:

1. Tell me about a challenge you confronted in the past.
2. What did you learn from the experience and what might you do differently?
3. Tell me how you resolved a crisis by working with team members.
4. What has been your greatest motivation?
5. Tell me about a mistake you made and how you handled it.

Behavior-based questions require candidates to share specific examples. A complete response to these types of questions would include a situation, action and result. If the candidate misses any of these in his response, prompt him to fill in the blanks. You can learn a lot about a candidate by his or her responses to these.

Problem-solving questions pose specific situations relevant to the position and ask the candidate how he would react so you can gain an understanding of the candidate's thought process. You can get a good feel for how resourceful and creative a candidate is with problem-solving questions. Examples of situational questions include:

- How would you deal with an irate customer?
- You find that project/product XYZ is behind schedule. How do you step up the team?

Some companies go so far as to use brain teasers or riddles to evaluate a candidate's approach to situations.

Regardless of what type of problem-solving questions you pose, you can expect a good candidate to:

- Assess and appreciate the scope of the problem

- Communicate assumptions
- Demonstrate quantitative analytical skills
- Address the question asked (You might make note if the candidate gets lost in the analysis and solves for a different question than what was asked.)

Culture-fit questions enable you to get an idea as to how the candidate will fit into your organization and corporate culture. Keep in mind the personalities already on your team and consider how the personality emerging during the interview will blend with those. These types of questions might include:

- Why did you choose this line of work?
- What gave you the greatest satisfaction in your last position?
- What inspires you?
- Describe the best boss you ever had.

In addition to preparing your list of questions, be prepared to sell the company to the candidate. What makes your company an attractive place to work to the best talent? What impressions do you want to leave with the candidate about your company? Be prepared to highlight the strengths and attributes of the company, but don't go overboard and make this the focus of the interview.

With the advance preparation in place, you will be well-equipped to conduct the interview thoroughly and efficiently. You are organized and relaxed, ready to find your new team member. Let your job description and ideal candidate definition serve as guidelines, but as with anything else, keep an open mind throughout the interview process.

Again, an important thing to remember is a good interviewee is not necessarily a good candidate and vice versa. I had a candidate years ago who was very nervous during the interview. I worked with him to prepare him to the best of my ability, but he was still nervous during the interview with the client and they were reluctant to hire him.

I told the hiring manager to look past the nervousness and really listen to the answers that were being given during the interview. The candidate did get the job, did extremely well in the position, and 14 years later is a vice president, which attests to his ability.

Do your homework. Be prepared for the interview. And be prepared to keep an open mind as well.

Chapter 3:

On the Spot

"Mediocrity knows nothing higher than itself, but talent instantly recognizes genius." – Arthur Conan Doyle.

Now that you've done all the preparation, you have a set of criteria in mind that your ideal candidate should possess. You will use the interview process to determine if the person being interviewed has the skills, capabilities and personal attributes that you envisioned.

A key component of your interview will be *listening* in order to determine the candidate's true competencies, compare the candidate to your vision of the ideal candidate, and later to distinguish between candidates. A general rule is that you should only spend 20 percent of the time talking, and 80 percent listening to the candidate's responses.

Most of your questions are geared toward gaining information in three basic areas:

- Can the candidate do the job?
- Will the candidate do the job well?
- What will it cost to hire this candidate?

First and foremost you need to assess the skills, education, experience and aptitude of the candidate. From there it is important to determine whether the candidate's interests and abilities match those required for the position as well as those of the company. It is also critical to evaluate how motivated the candidate is and if he has the personal qualities necessary for the job. Finally, when considering a new hire, you are working within a budget. You will need to assess the cost of hiring the candidate, including salary, benefits and training.

Fine tuning your questions

Again, you want to employ a variety of interview questions in order to get a good feel for the candidate's abilities and personality to ensure a good fit. I like to have a number of different questions in several categories: fact-finding, creative-thinking, problem-solving and behavioral. There are many questions you'll need to stay away from, for legal reasons, but we'll get to those in the next chapter. Asking the wrong questions can land you in court, but for now, let's focus on the types of questions that will help you address the above basic areas.

It's a good idea to begin with some open-ended questions to enable the candidate to exhibit some control. This will help him feel more at ease so he can more easily move on to more detailed questions later.

Open-ended questions

- Tell me about yourself.
- What was your first job?
- What's your greatest accomplishment?
- What has been your greatest challenge and what did you learn from it?
- What is the difference between a good position and an excellent one?
- Where do you see yourself in five years?
- How are you unique?

In addition to open-ended questions, you will want to use some specific questions, depending on the key competencies on which you need to focus. The way in which a person has handled certain situations in the past can give you a valid perspective as to how that person will perform under similar circumstances. Some questions to help elicit specific examples of past performance include:

- Tell me how you worked with _____?
- Describe _____'s management style?
- What did you learn in your current/previous position that has prepared you for greater responsibilities?
- Describe a key relationship that you had to work to maintain.
- Tell me about a situation in which you had to make a critical decision.
- Give me an example of a challenge you confronted and how you resolved it.
- Describe a successful group effort you took part in.
- Describe a typical day in your work life.
- How do you learn from others?

Look for how the candidate expresses himself. Note his convictions. Drawing out stories will give you an idea of the candidate's motivations and passions. This can be critical in hiring. That's why I find it's a good idea to do a phone interview first and get a sense of this, but it's equally important to look for it in the face-to-face interview.

Leadership Competencies

Kells Associates raised the issue of identifying key leadership competencies: knowledge, skills and attitudes that are relevant to your company's success.

You'll want to build some questions around these areas. See the list on the next page for key areas to address.

Sample Leadership Competencies
(Adopted from The Career Architect Development Planner)

Action Orientation	Approachability
Boss Relationships	Business Acumen
Career Ambition	Caring About Direct Reports
Compassion	Composure
Conflict Management	Creativity
Customer Focus	Decision Making
Delegation	Developing Direct Reports
Drive for Results	Managing Diversity
Ethics and Values	Functional / Technical Skills
Hiring and Staffing	Humor
Informing	Innovation Management
Integrity and Trust	Interpersonal Savvy
Listening	Managerial Courage
Measurement	Motivating Others
Negotiating	Organizational Agility
Organizing	Dealing with Paradox

Patience	Peer Relationships
Perseverance	Personal Learning
Planning	Political Savvy
Presentation Skills	Problem Solving
Process Management	Self-Development
Self-Knowledge	Strategic Agility
Building Effective Teams	Technical Learning
Time Management	TQM / Re-Engineering
Understanding Others	Managing Vision and Purpose
Work / Life Balance	Written Communications

Management-related questions

- How do you measure the performance of your subordinates?
- Have you ever had to fire someone? How did you handle it?
- What is your management style?
- Describe your most difficult experience as a manager.
- What would your staff say about your management style?
- Tell me about your best boss. What made him or her your best boss?

Sales-specific questions

- Why are you successful at sales?
- How do you persuade a reluctant customer?

- Describe your most successful sale.
- How would you sell me this pen?
- How do you stay motivated?
- What has been your greatest challenge in meeting sales quotas?
- Describe a typical week in your most recent sales position.
- How do you overcome objections?
- How do you handle a face-to-face challenge?

For sales I like to ask what's been their exposure to sales jobs. If they had parents who were in sales, relatives, family friends, a lot of times there would be discussion about work around the dinner table or at barbeques, holiday get-togethers, etc. The reality of the job and the industry were likely discussed so the candidate would already have some familiarity with them. He has some idea of what he's in for and you are aware that he has this added insight.

The same thing holds true for engineers, technology people, etc. Any past exposure, even peripherally, could prove insightful.

Each person interviewing the candidate should have a separate list of questions to ask, but these questions should be consistent among candidate interviews to allow for more accurate comparisons. Agree on a standard set of questions for each interviewer.

You may want to include a peer interview. This can help round out a company's perspective on the candidate. The employee can take stock of the candidate and report to his boss. Candidates tend to be more at ease with peers, so the employee is likely to get a more objective view of the candidate. But keep in mind that it's a two-way street: candidates will likely get a more accurate picture of the company from someone who works there rather than someone presenting only what he wants the candidate to know.

Peer interviews can be especially useful for team-based organizations and can help boost morale. Employees involved in the hiring process generally feel appreciated and that they have more of a stake in the company. They have a vested interest in the new hire's success, and the new hire, in turn, can start work knowing he has peers who support him.

Conducting effective interviews

As a representative for the company, your appearance and demeanor reflects the corporate image. Indeed, your entire interview process indicates the value your company places on its people. You can project a strong, positive corporate image by conducting a professional interview, communicating fairly and honestly, and basing your hiring decisions on a thorough evaluation of each candidate.

Have someone welcome and accompany the candidate to the interview site. Take a moment to help the candidate feel comfortable and at ease so you get a true understanding of their competencies and personality. Ask some icebreaker questions or make small talk about the weather, the drive etc. Some easy examples include: "Did you have any trouble finding our office?" or "Would you like some coffee?"

This is also a good time to acknowledge that you went to the same school, belong to the same association or have something in common. Address the candidate by first name to help quickly establish a good rapport. This preliminary exchange also allows you to see the candidate's general communication style.

Begin the interview with a brief summary of the position, including major responsibilities, reporting structure, key performance criteria and any challenges you foresee. This will enable the candidate to provide relevant responses. Take a moment to make the candidate aware of what you do and how it relates to the position for which he is interviewing. Be thorough, but mindful not to dominate the interview time with a lengthy introduction.

Your basic questions should be consistent from interview to interview so you can effectively compare candidate responses. Ask general, open-ended questions as discussed in chapter two. When more information is needed, probe to clarify with specific examples. Stay on track but don't let your enthusiasm for a candidate cloud your judgment. If you're asking too many questions to confirm your "gut feelings", back up for a moment and ask a more challenging question, such as *give me an example of when things did not go as planned and how you handled it*.

Be flexible. Plan your questions, but don't be afraid to improvise when something comes up in the interview you want to pursue further. Be responsive to the candidate's replies, and you may find that new questions arise from those answers.

Feel free to take notes. You may want to summarize the candidate's strengths and weaknesses for comparison with other candidates later on.

Always invite the candidate to ask questions about the job or the company. You can gain added insight about the candidate by the questions he asks. Good questions can show initiative and motivation, show that the candidate has been paying attention, and give you an idea of where his true interests lie.

Do not feel the need to fill the silence! Allow time for thinking and reflection by the candidate and take note of his demeanor during these breaks in dialogue.

Be forthright. Don't be afraid to talk about the challenges facing the position or the company. Ultimately you want everyone on the same page. If the candidate is hired and doesn't have an understanding of the true situation, you may lose him quickly. Be open about the challenges but use positive words and help him buy into the situation.

At the same time, you can be forthright about the positives and the things that make your company unique. One company I recruit for tells people that if you do 18 months with their company, you have the potential to be pursued by other companies. They don't want people to leave; they want people to understand that they're invested in their success, so much so that their employees are sought after by other firms. Their company offers the opportunity to grow and develop and it's important for the candidates to know that.

The dynamics of body language

Non-verbal cues can speak volumes. You can discreetly observe the candidate in the reception area even before the interview starts.

During an interview, *how* the person responds can be as important as the response itself. It has been said that 60-80% of a message is communicated through body language rather than verbal communication. You can gain a fair amount of insight from the candidate's body language, facial expressions and communication style.

It is thought that we form opinions about a new person we meet within seconds. Much of what is communicated in those first few seconds is nonverbal. You'll note right away how the person carries himself. Does he show poise and confidence, head up, shoulders back, or is he slouched, appearing uncertain and under confident?

One early indicator can seem like a cliché, but it's true: A firm handshake immediately warms you to a person and gives the impression of strength and confidence. Look to this element of style in both genders as an early indication of the candidate's self-assurance.

Another vital component of any interpersonal encounter is eye contact. Focused eye contact not only indicates confidence, but shows that the candidate is attentive and engaged. Good eye contact should be maintained throughout the interview. Less eye contact could indicate lack of confidence, uneasiness, evasiveness, and even lack of interest in the position.

Head and face movements can also indicate the level of engagement. They can indicate active listening when they correspond appropriately to what is being said. For instance, a head nod at something relevant and smiles and other facial expressions are suitable at times. The head, as well as the upper body leaning forward, can also indicate interest and a positive reaction to what is being said.

Crossed arms can indicate reluctance or defensiveness as they establish a sense of separation. Crossed arms may also be exhibited by someone who is physically cold, so be sure to take this signal in context.

Perhaps because hands contain more nerve connections to the brain than many parts of the body, they tend to be particularly expressive. They can be used in illustration, for emphasis and for specific signals such as the positive thumbs-up or OK sign. What some people may not know is that the hands can also "leak" unconscious signals, such as when interacting with paper, pens or paper clips, can indicate feelings of doubt, deceit, openness, expectation, etc.

Steepling, or having the fingertips of each hand touching, is thought to reflect elevated thinking. You may notice this when a candidate is trying to make connections that explain. While steepling the fingers upward often indicates thoughtfulness, steepling outward in the direction of another person may also indicate a barrier. Interwoven, clenched fingers may indicate anxiety or frustration.

Touching or scratching the nose while speaking is thought to be a sign of exaggeration, while scratching the neck points toward doubt. Tugging on the ear can indicate self-comforting and indecision. Generally people finger different parts of the body in an effort to provide self comfort, but ear tugging is thought to indicate related contemplation.

Although leg and feet body language is more difficult to fake than some of those mentioned, keep in mind that when someone sits for a half hour or more, they are likely to change leg positions simply from a standpoint of comfort. In addition, men and women tend to sit differently, which should also be taken into consideration.

Curiously, the direction in which the knees are pointed tends to correspond with the level of interest. A person sitting will unconsciously direct their knees toward the subject of interest, and on the other hand will naturally direct them away from something that is uninteresting or intimidating. Feet follow a similar pattern.

While crossed legs are thought to indicate a lack of interest or caution and uncrossed legs are thought to indicate a sense of openness, keep in mind that these naturally vary with gender. Again, if legs are crossed, consider where the knee is pointed to help determine the level of enthusiasm. The figure-4 leg crossing, with the ankle resting on the opposite knee however, tends to exhibit confidence. Take other signals into account as this posture can indicate independence or stubbornness. Finally, legs crossed at the ankles are thought to indicate defensiveness and intertwined legs, usually a female posture, can suggest insecurity.

While many signals can give the impression of boredom or anxiety, it is important to take into consideration the context of the meeting. Be wary and take body language in context. Body language in one situation might not mean the same as in another. For example, someone scratching their nose or eye might actually have an itch or irritation, rather than being evasive or tired. Look for repetition of body language signals for a more reliable means of interpretation. In addition there may be cultural differences in body language signals, such as personal space inclinations, which can vary among cultures.

Some people will work to control their body language in order to project the desired image. A firm handshake and good eye contact are two of the easiest and most easily controlled elements. However, an effort to exude confidence where there is little is likely to be temporary, and this is all the more reason to look for clusters of indicators and avoid a more superficial check based on isolated signals.

In addition, sales people are often taught to mirror or match their body language with that of the person with whom they are speaking. This helps to build a rapport and put people at ease. It encourages trust. Though some mirroring may be conscious, it is not necessarily deceptive, and can be effective in engaging a person and building trust.

As a general rule, positive body language includes:

- Moving or leaning in closer
- Relaxed, uncrossed limbs
- Consistent eye contact
- A genuine smile

Negative body language includes:

- Moving or leaning away from the interviewer
- Crossed arms or legs
- Looking away to the side
- Feet pointed away or towards an exit
- Rubbing/scratching the nose, eyes or back of neck

Again, the above are general rules to provide basic insight, but a single cue can mean different things. It's important to take notice of numerous behavioral cues from the candidate and take them in context. Keep in mind that some people exhibit certain behaviors regularly as part of their personality as well, so be sure to consider the overall picture rather than isolated cues.

Test drive

You may want to host a mock sales call. This provides an opportunity for the candidate to demonstrate their sales skills and for you to evaluate their performance. "Sell me this pen." You can see how the candidate:

- Builds rapport
- Demonstrates product knowledge
- Educates the customer
- Presents himself
- Handles objections

I always think back to an interview I was having with a vice president years ago who handed me a pen and said, "Sell me this pen." I'm a gadget guy so I happened to have with me a pen I'd purchased that had a recorder in it. It was expensive for the time, maybe around $85 in 1995 or so.

I started in sales mode with his pen, not so much selling as inquiring into his needs, asking a lot of questions about how he uses pens. I then brought out my high-tech recording pen and asked more questions about whether or not he ever had a need to record a meeting, ran out of ink and could have used a tape recorder, questions relating to the benefits of my pen.

I got the job and now whenever someone gives this example of "sell me this pen," I think of that moment, but the point is it's a good interviewing technique. That vice president interviewing me was a good manager and a good interviewer and was able to put me in a position where he could see for himself some of what I had to offer.

Another thing I suggest clients do is have the candidate produce a writing sample. Ask them a question and have them type out a one- to two-paragraph response on a computer. Something simple such as, "Tell me about your biggest personal or professional accomplishment."

A cover letter can indicate the candidate's ability to communicate, but it may be a template. A writing sample produced during the interview cannot be borrowed from another source. It's not as important what the person says in his writing sample as much as how they articulate their ideas and demonstrate written communication skills. Look at their grammar, sentence structure, syntax, and etcetera.

You may also want to have the candidate sit and watch a person in the position for a half hour or so. This enables him to see what's really involved. It can make or break the candidate's desire for the job, but ultimately it's better to find out before the person is hired if he's truly willing and motivated to do the job.

Questions I like to end with include:

- What are your personal and professional goals? Are they written down?
- How often do you refer to them?
- What's the last book you read? What's the last professional book you read?
- What newspapers, periodicals, and blogs do you read?
- How do you stay current in your industry?

End on a positive note. Thank the candidate for taking the time to meet with you and provide a reasonable expectation of the next steps. Will there be additional interviews, and if so, with whom and when? When and by whom should the candidate expect the next contact?

Overall, be sure to have a standard set of questions and use a consistent format for all interviews. This will enable you to more accurately assess candidates and helps protect against discrimination and unfair hiring practices.

Chapter 4:
The Legal Perspective

While you're focused on finding and hiring the best person for the position, don't lose sight of the legal issues that loom in the background throughout the hiring process. It still amazes me that in today's litigious society so many hiring still ask questions during an interview that are not appropriate or are outright discriminatory.

Many companies, and even some recruiters, write ads that exclude certain people or groups. I once saw an ad that said the company was looking for someone in a certain age range and actually stated "good looking." I've gone so far as to call some of these companies and offer to help them rewrite these types of ads, but so far none of them have taken me up on the offer.

Greg Hare has been an employment lawyer at Ogletree Deakins since 1991. He assists companies with human resources and employment-related litigation matters, including wrongful termination claims, sexual harassment, employment discrimination, employment contracts, trade secrets, and non-compete agreements. Mr. Hare encourages companies to develop proactive human resources strategies that are designed to minimize exposure to costly litigation and disputes. This commonly includes conducting comprehensive employment law compliance audits, employment policy design and review, management training and counseling, and simulated problem solving workshops.

Mr. Hare says, "Probably the single biggest mistake employers make in the hiring process is not training recruiters and hiring managers in employment law."

Employment disputes are a fast-growing area of litigation and miss-steps can be problematic. From job posting to rejection letters, there are several things to keep in mind to avoid legal concerns down the road. Most important, know that the Equal Employment Opportunity (EEO) laws prohibit discrimination against job applicants on the basis of age, race, color, religion, sex, disability or national origin.

Job description

In addition to providing a written account of the position to be filled, the job description is a legal document that should protect both the company and the person who eventually fills the position.

It is important to avoid language in your job description and ad that may be questionable or discriminatory. Terms, such as "energetic, youthful candidates" or "recent graduates preferred", could be seen as age discriminatory. As mentioned in Chapter 1, be certain the education level and experience requirements are truly necessary in order to do the job. To avoid age discrimination, list a minimum years of experience required rather than setting an upper limit.

You may want to include terms of employment which should follow any existing company policies and be approved by your legal advisor. Use inclusive language such as "salesperson" rather than "salesman." Clearly define any essential tasks of the position so there is no suggestion of disability discrimination.

Three things to keep in mind to avoid legal issues with your job description:

1. Keep it real. Be sure that requirements stated in the job are just that: required.

2. Don't imply future advancement. Describe the job at hand only and don't suggest that the position being offered is a stepping-stone to a future position.

3. Keep it simple. Use commonly understood terms rather than trying to dress up the position with flowery language. If you're looking for a trash collector say that, rather than advertising for a "refuse-maintenance engineer."

Interviewing

It is critical that everyone involved in the interview process follow legal guidelines. The best way to be certain you are fully compliant is to ask only questions relating to the job, eliminating any room for bias.

You absolutely cannot ask any questions relating in any way to age, sex, marital status/family, race or religion. For instance in regard to age, you cannot ask what year the candidate was born, how old he is, or when he graduated high school. You can verify if he is of minimum age required for the position, which is generally over the age of 18, or in the case of a bartender, 21.

In regard to sex and family arrangements, you cannot ask anything relating to the sex of the applicant, how many children he has or plans to have, marital status, childcare arrangements, spouse's occupation, spouse's salary or health coverage through spouse. You cannot ask what the appropriate title is, such as Dr., Miss, or Mrs.

You can ask if the applicant has relatives already employed by the company. You can also state what time the work day begins and ask whether there are any specific commitments that would prevent the candidate from starting at the required time.

You cannot ask any race-oriented questions such as the color of the applicant's skin or specific race. You also cannot require that a photo be affixed to the application form. You cannot ask what country the candidate is from or where he was born. Nor can you ask these questions regarding his parents. You cannot ask what language is spoken at home. You can verify the work/visa status and what language the applicant is fluent in as is required for the position.

You cannot ask the candidate's religious affiliation and whether or not he attends some method of worship regularly. You cannot ask which religious holidays the candidate observes.

If the candidate has an obvious disability you can ask if he can perform the essential job-related functions, but again be certain these are essential functions. You cannot ask the candidate if he has a disability or the nature and severity of the disability. You cannot inquire whether the applicant has ever filed a workers' compensation claim. You cannot ask about recent or past surgeries and dates or past medical problems.

Furthermore, criminal background questions are also limited. You cannot ask if the candidate spent time in jail or has been arrested. In most cases you are permitted to inquire about convictions if they are job-related, but check with legal counsel as this may vary in some jurisdictions.

You cannot ask if the applicant owns or rents a home or what town he lives in. You can ask if the address on the resume is the best place to contact the candidate.

Other questions to avoid include those related to height or weight, veteran status, discharge status or branch of service, though you can ask about training received in the military as it relates to the specific position. And finally, during the interview stage you cannot ask whom to contact in case of an emergency. This question is only applicable upon hiring the candidate.

The following table provides guidelines to help you distinguish between legal and discriminatory interview questions. Keep in mind any question that is not specifically job related may be interpreted as unlawful.

Subject	What you CANNOT ask	What you CAN ask
Name	What is your maiden name or any previously used name? What is your preferences regarding Miss, Mrs. or Ms.?	For access purposes, are any work records are under another name.
Age	What is your date of birth? What is your age?	If hired, can you provide proof of age/submit a work permit?
Birthplace	Where were you born? Where were your parents born?	
Arrests & convictions	Have you ever been arrested? Have you ever been charged with a crime?	Have you been convicted of any crime? Are there any felony charges pending? If so, provide details.
Religion/ Creed	Anything related to religious affiliation, denomination, church, parish, pastor, minister, rabbi or religious holidays observed.	Are you available to work on Saturdays or Sundays if needed (Only if applicable to the job)?
Race	Anything related to race, complexion, color of skin, etc.	

Subject	What you CANNOT ask	What you CAN ask
Gender	Anything even remotely related to gender.	
Citizenship	In what country were you born? Have you/family members become naturalized citizens & when?	Are you a citizen of the US? If not, are you prevented from becoming lawfully employed because of visa or immigration status? If hired, can you submit proof of citizenship or employment eligibility?
Residence	With whom do you reside? Do you own a home or rent? Names and relationships of people residing with you.	What is your present address? How long have you resided at this address? What was your former address and how long did you reside there?
Military record	What is the type, conditions or dates of your military discharge? Anything about experience in other than US armed forces or state militia.	Are you a veteran of the US armed forces or state militia? If so, describe any training or education received while in the military.

Subject	What you CANNOT ask	What you CAN ask
Relatives	List names and addresses of relatives to be notified in case of emergency.	Do you have any relatives already employed by this company? If so, please list their names.
Disabilities & health	Are you handicapped? Do you have a disability? Have you ever been treated for any of the following diseases...? Have you ever filed a Worker's Compensation claim? What is your height/weight? Are you on any medications?	Are you able to perform the essential tasks and duties of the position as they have been explained to you?
National origin or language	What is your ancestry, lineage, national origin, descent, parentage or nationality, or that of parents or spouse? What is your native language and how was fluency acquired?	What languages do you read, speak or write fluently (only if job related)?

Subject	What you CANNOT ask	What you CAN ask
Marital/Family status	What is your marital status: spouse's name, employment, etc.? What is your maiden name or preference among Miss, Mrs., Ms.? What is the number and age of your children? Plans to have children? Are you pregnant? What are your child care arrangements?	Are there any commitments or responsibilities that would hinder you with work attendance requirements?
Organizations	List any social organizations, clubs, societies and lodges to which you belong.	List memberships in any professional, trade, or other organizations you consider relevant to your ability to perform the job.
Credit rating	Any questions relating to credit rating, charge accounts, car ownership, etc.	Can you be bonded?(if applicable)

The Americans with Disabilities Act (ADA) prohibits discrimination against qualified people with disabilities. In addition to the questions, the interview process itself must be deemed non-discriminatory. The interview must be accessible to people with disabilities.

Do not automatically assume that the candidate needs assistance. Ask your questions in a straightforward manner.

Despite the lengthy list, Mr. Hare states, "There is no such thing as asking illegal questions. What is illegal is making employment-related decisions based on impermissible factors. The list of impermissible factors keeps growing. "

He recommends you stick to the job description and specific requirements: "Can you fulfill the requirements of the job?", not "Will you need to stay home with sick kids?"

He further suggests that some companies are so fearful they have become robotic in their approach to interviewing, following a script. There is nothing wrong with getting to know someone in a conversational manner. You just need to be business appropriate.

Reference checks

Employment reference laws limit what you can ask of a candidate's past employers. Essentially you can ask:

1. Dates of employment
2. Job title
3. Salary
4. Duties performed

You can ask the candidate to sign a waiver which would allow you to check references. The potential candidate's signature ensures that he will not hold you accountable for any information provided by the former employer.

It is also important to check references in order to avoid lawsuits arising from negligent hiring or failure to exercise reasonable care when selecting new employees. If you do not attempt reasonable inquiries regarding the candidate, and the candidate is hired and causes injury, you may be found responsible. Attempting to check references ensures Due Diligence, which protects you from legal exposure.

Mr. Hare advises standard background checks at the national, state and county level. "State laws present a complex web of knowledge. It is imperative that hiring managers know particular state laws."

Some companies rely on a professional third party such as a recruiter to handle reference checks. Recruiters are able to gather the information more objectively and provide a more accurate picture of the candidate's skills in relation to the job description. In addition, recruiters do so many reference checks that their experience in handling this important aspect of the hiring process may help them get more out of the reference check than someone less experienced at asking the questions.

Rejection letters

The most important thing to remember in writing a rejection letter is that you are telling the candidate he is not a good match for the position, not that he is not a good candidate. This not only sends the appropriate message, it leaves the door open for continued contact. I often check back with candidates weeks, months and even years later and sometimes identify them as a good candidate for another position.

If a candidate has come in for an interview, they deserve the benefit of a letter and/or phone call thanking them for their time. That said, employee lawsuits tend to increase during a recession. As frustration mounts, more applicants may read more into the rejection letter than you intended.

While you may want to maintain good will with the applicant that you are rejecting, some wording in rejection letters may be grounds for a lawsuit. Check with legal counsel to be certain your rejection letters avoid any legal pitfalls and do not rile the recipient.

Three Don'ts of rejection letters:

1. Don't say anything about the experience and qualifications of the candidate, other candidates, or person who may have been hired for the position. A lawyer for a rejected applicant may ask for the applications of the top candidates to compare qualifications.

2. Don't give the impression that you will keep the resume on file for future reference, or that you will contact the candidate if a future position becomes available; you may not. If another candidate is hired in the future, a lawyer may again ask to compare the qualifications of that candidate with the resume you were supposed to have on file.

3. Don't use words such as "unfortunately" or "we're sorry" as they may fuel the rejected applicant's negative point of view.

Three Do's of rejection letters:

1. Make the letter brief and direct.

2. Thank the candidate for applying for your position. Be pleasant and polite.

3. Send the letter soon after the hiring decision has been made so the candidate is not building up anxiety or resentment waiting for a decision.

Sample rejection letter:

Dear (Name):

Thank you for submitting your resume in response to our ad for a sales executive. We are unable to offer you the position.

We appreciate your interest in XYZ Company and wish you much success in your job search.

Sincerely,

Discrimination – or perceived discrimination – can take place in any number of places throughout the hiring process. While you have the right to seek, evaluate and hire the person you think most appropriate for the position, the process is not without legal pitfalls. Limit your company's exposure to these hiring practice legalities with careful thought to the policies you have in place.

Mr. Hare counsels his clients, "No matter what the regulations provide, no matter how complex the web of regulations, don't forgo common sense."

He tells the story of a client years ago that hired an employee for its merchandising company in Wisconsin. The position required the employee to set up merchandising displays with a small group of employees during off-hours.

The first level criminal background check was ambiguous. Weeks later after a more thorough background check it was learned that the employee had served jail time for assaulting his boss, and the company subsequently fired him.

The employee in question sued for wrongful discharge. The Wisconsin Labor Board planned to take the case to hearing, stating that the prior incident did not directly relate to the individual's present position. The Labor Board later postponed the hearing indefinitely, and after much prodding admitted that the individual had been subsequently arrested for running a meth lab.

"The moral of the story is follow your gut," Mr. Hare says. "It's easier to defend a wrongful discharge suit than a wrongful death arising from a bad hire. I tell all my clients, when in doubt, do what's best for your business."

Chapter 5:

Evaluate for Success

Recruiter Karen Holt tells the story of a candidate she had who was in the final interview stage, meeting with the client's vice president. The candidate was perfect. Karen expected the job was hers. Instead, the candidate was sent away after just 15 minutes with the vice president.

"I don't like her," was all Karen could initially get out of the vice president. Upon further prodding, Karen was able to discover that the candidate wore the same perfume as the vice president's ex-wife, and the 15 minute interview was the end of the candidate's encounter with the client.

It happens. Sometimes an emotional factor triggers a response that is less than practical in the evaluation process, but you've done your homework. You've asked all the proper questions. How *should* you determine which, if any, of the candidates you've met with would make the ideal match?

Investing in the pre-hire evaluation process will increase your chances of choosing the right candidate. The closer you can associate the evaluations to the job requirements, the more likely you will be to determine the right candidate.

First impressions

First impressions influence our immediate attitude toward an individual and often set the groundwork for the relationship that will follow. According to *Psychology Today* (http://www.psychologytoday.

com/articles/200405/the-first-impression) our brains develop first impressions based on a collection of various factors involved in a new experience. How accurate these impressions are depend both on the observer as well as the person being observed.

Is the individual neat, appropriately attired and seemingly confident? Does he make eye contact, have a sincere smile and have a firm handshake? Does he appear to be presenting himself in the best possible manner?

Many of these factors influence our perception of the candidate's competency, approachability and likability. Especially in positions requiring a high level of sociability, such as in sales or management, the initial impressions at an interview could be influential in your evaluation of a candidate.

While it's natural to have these reactions to a candidate, it's important to defer judgment until all factors – including experience, credentials, reference checks, etc. – can be fully taken into account. The first impression is only one aspect of the complete picture and should be evaluated accordingly.

An important thing to consider when evaluating first impressions is your own decision-making process. Are you quick to react instinctively or do you take the time to more fully contemplate all factors?

As in the case of the perfume story, an emotional reaction was triggered and an otherwise suitable candidate was turned away. I remember a client I once had that was very concerned with whether or not the candidate had the right dimple in their tie. That superficial methodology had very little to do with the reality of the individual's capabilities.

An awareness of how you tend to react to people, the type of people you are naturally drawn to, and knowledge of what has worked for you in the past can help in your evaluation of a first impression. You will be able to be more objective in an interview if you are aware of your own decision-making process and do not let your first impressions steer your line of questions. Remain objective, keep the interview fair, and keep the questions consistent with those you're using to interview all the candidates for the position.

Finding the right fit for both candidate and company

First, have Human Resources follow up on any fact-checking or background items you may have noted during the interview. Also watch for candidate follow up. They should send a thank you note and any additional information you may have requested.

Beyond that there are many factors that need to be evaluated when finding the candidate that is the right fit for your company. Depending on the position, your corporate culture and your company goals, some may be more important than others. Some of the major areas to consider include:

Evaluation Categories

Communication Skills

Presentation

Oral

- Interpersonal
- Professional
- Technical

Written

Listening ability

Personal

- Motivation

- Work ethic
- Attention to detail
- Integrity
- Energy level
- Identification w/management
- Identification w/peers
- Initiative
- Ability to learn
- Self-organization

Decision-making ability

- Thorough analysis
- Decisiveness
- Risk taking
- Creativity

Knowledge/Skills

- Education
- Years of experience
- Technical knowledge

Management

- Planning
- Organization

- Delegation
- Coordination
- Monitoring
- Subordinate development

Interpersonal

- Sensitivity
- Persuasiveness
- Tenacity
- Drive
- Teamwork
- Customer service

Impact

- Leadership
- Adaptability
- Flexibility
- Negotiating
- Rapport building
- Team building
- Independence
- Problem solving
- Resilience

Career path

- Ambition
- Willingness to learn
- Self development
- Goals

When you are evaluating your top candidates, there's more to consider than whether the candidate is *qualified* to do the job. You need to also consider if he's *motivated* to do the job and what makes him motivated to do the job. Does he have the personal drive, initiative and resolve to accomplish your goals based on your terms? Is he motivated by compensation, benefits, family concerns, location, career advancement, etc., and will your corporate culture, structure and compensation program meet those criteria?

The candidate is thinking about what's in it for him. From his point of view what's important to him is clearly more important than what's important to the company. You need to evaluate whether what you have to offer meets his personal objectives to ensure a match that will prove mutually beneficial and keep him happy and, therefore, productive.

At this point in the process you may also want to consider what makes him motivated to make a move to your job. This is best evaluated by identifying the candidate's career wound. Typically, unless the move is simply being made for more money or responsibility, there are four key reasons why an employee might be motivated to look for another position:

1. Change in compensation
2. Change in management or corporate structure

3. Change in responsibility/workload

4. Perception of financial instability within the company

This is where a recruiter has an obvious advantage in the evaluation process. A candidate will naturally be more open about his true motivation for a move with a recruiter - an objective third party - than a member of the company with which he is trying to gain a position.

Another thing to consider when you're evaluating the top performers is whether you truly want a top performer. While your initial reaction is usually "of course," keep in mind that top performers are a different breed from the average hire and managing them is therefore different as well.

Top performers question everything, whether financial rewards, recognition, corporate goals or otherwise. They are never quite completely satisfied. They are driven to outperform and outpace their peers, which can put some people off. They may even get in each other's way and their exceptional relationship building abilities can be seen as political. What's more, their extreme customer-oriented advocacy can eat into the company's profits.

These are a few examples of how positive traits of top performers may be perceived as negative. You have to determine whether or not your company management and corporate culture is equipped to handle these perceptions should they arise. You must objectively look at your company to determine if these types of individuals are indeed a good fit.

I have also found in 20 years of recruiting that often the number one candidate does not end up being the candidate hired. Someone who is the primary candidate in the beginning may lose their luster during the search and hiring process. Cracks and weaknesses begin to show. Also, sometimes you'll find that the perfect person becomes a high-maintenance situation and that may not be in your best interest. It's important that you not pin all your hopes on one candidate, but rather have several top candidates from which you can choose.

Remember - you don't want to hire the best interviewer. You want to hire the best person for the job. Not every candidate or every person is going to be perfect. You have to determine what percentage of skills sets and attributes you are willing to accept.

The concept of the perfect candidate is illusive at best. In recruiting we call it the purple squirrel. There is no such thing. As hard and long as you look, you will not find it. It's like the *Cheers* episode in which Sam, Norm, Cliff and several others take Frazier Snipe hunting, only to make Frazier look foolish because, as Sam explains to Diane, Snipes don't exist.

Sometimes you think you've found the perfect candidate, but no matter how thorough you've been or how many obstacles you've addressed, there's still a surprise in store. Several years ago a candidate went through a very arduous interview process with a client. The process took more than eight weeks with six interviews with members of the management team, testing, presentations, references and a written example of a sales plan. The conditional offer and salary negotiations were finalized.

On the day the "perfect candidate" was given the official offer and he accepted, the team took him to lunch to celebrate. The candidate thought the process was over and let his guard down. When the waitress came to take his order he spoke to her disrespectfully. The offer was rescinded because our client did not want someone who behaved in that manner representing them.

You can never be completely sure. At the same time, you don't have to settle for a lesser candidate, but the "perfect candidate" – the purple squirrel – is not going to be found. Finding people who are not perfectly perfect is okay – so long as they're respectful to those around them as our story illustrates!

In working with another company that had an inside sales position, I was able to find four candidates which I presented in order of my conviction that each could do the job. My number four candidate was very accomplished as far as experience, but during the interview process I had uncovered that he seemed to be high maintenance. When the client asked why he wasn't my number one candidate I explained this to them. I felt there were some red flags, that he'd need hand holding and would end up being a drain on time.

The client ultimately hired him but eventually found that I was right. The new hire's employment was terminated a year and a half later and my client was no longer surprised that the employee tended to change jobs every six to eight months

There's an old adage that says "look for individuals with past success". This is important because these individuals know how to achieve and how to work through adversity and overcome obstacles.

At the same time, experience isn't everything. Look for individuals whose traits and values are in line with your company. A high level of motivation, for example, may outweigh experience and be a good indicator of the candidate's ability to perform on the job.

There is so much to consider. To help you organize your thoughts and assess each candidate, I recommend using an applicant evaluation form. The use of a form will help you compare candidates more readily and help different interviewers compare notes.

The evaluation form[1] on the next page is just one example. My company uses a much more detailed quantification format which we tailor for the clients with which we work.

---

1   Rich, L. (2003, March) *Tools of the Trade: Conducting Effective Interviews*. Paper presented at NEHRA North Shore Breakfast, Duxbury, MA.

Candidate Evaluation Form

Candidate Name: _____
Position: _____ **Date:** _____
Location: _____ **Manager:** _____
Referral Source: _____

SCALE (based on qualifications)
5: Exceptional
4: Better than average
3: Fully qualified
2: Less than fully qualified
1: Unacceptable
0: Not observed

Background	5	4	3	2	1	0
Sales success *(regularly achieves quota, wins trips, etc.)*	5	4	3	2	1	0
Telephone cold calling	5	4	3	2	1	0
Prospecting	5	4	3	2	1	0
Hunter	5	4	3	2	1	0
Presenting to senior management	5	4	3	2	1	0
Initiative	5	4	3	2	1	0
Quick	5	4	3	2	1	0
Fun	5	4	3	2	1	0
High integrity	5	4	3	2	1	0
Interpersonal skills	5	4	3	2	1	0
Stress tolerance	5	4	3	2	1	0
Verbal communications	5	4	3	2	1	0
Presentations	5	4	3	2	1	0

OVERALL IMPRESSION

____ Exceptional   ____ Strong   ____ Capable   ____ Weak   ____ Very Weak

RECOMMENDATIONS

____ Hire   ____ Do Not Hire   ____ Refer to _____

_____   _____
Interviewer   Date

Background and reference checks

With all the legal issues involved, background and reference checks may seem like a mere formality, but they are indeed critical components of the hiring process. Personal references are generally not a very effective use of time. Rather, contact professional references who can give you better, more valuable insight into the candidate's professional life.

Clearly you would like to verify factual matters such as dates and titles. Various surveys suggest that as much as 40-50% of resumes include errors or outright fraud in factual data. It's worth the time to check out the details.

Essentially, you can lawfully ask:

5. Dates of employment
6. Job title
7. Salary
8. Duties performed

However, you can ask the candidate to sign a waiver allowing you to check references. The candidate's signature ensures that he will not hold you accountable for any information provided by the former employer.

Ideally, you would like insight into qualitative issues, such as performance, strengths and weaknesses. Due to the concerns over liabilities, many employers will not comment on job performance and will only verify dates of employment, job title and salary. In some cases, 900-phone numbers have been established to provide automated information regarding dates and titles.

One way around the challenge of gathering past performance insight is to try and talk with the candidate's former supervisor or coworkers. Coworkers are generally more inclined to speak freely. If that is not possible, you may try professional networking. Again, this is where a recruiter has a huge advantage in that recruiters have a broad network and knowledge of the key industry players.

I always recommend that clients seek specific written references of former managers or supervisors. One prominent recruiter I know even suggests reaching out to the candidate's best friend, as this person may be able to better indicate what's prompting the candidate to make a move and what his real motivations are.

Investigate social media

At this point in time the population at large should be quite familiar with the implications of everything they post on social media. You can only hope the candidates you're considering for your position conduct themselves in a reasonable manner on all fronts, but it's still considered worth your time to explore these areas further.

Indeed, entire companies and products exist to help you do just that. Depending on the time and money you put into this, you can get a detailed look at someone's comprehensive web presence.

Again, there are many factors to consider when evaluating a candidate. It is definitely worthwhile to take a look at your own evaluation process and then assess the candidate based on your objective criteria. If someone is not a good fit, consider why they are not a good fit and use that insight in future interviews. Your evaluation process will continue to evolve with your company.

Chapter 6:

Negotiations: The Art of the Deal

You've found your ideal candidate and you're ready to make the offer. Now you have to determine a compensation package that will make this match mutually acceptable for both you and the candidate. With a positive salary negotiation, both you and your new hire will be ready to embark on a successful long-term relationship. Keeping in mind that the interview process is a two-way street and that you have an important position to fill, the question remains, can you fill your need at a cost that will make a return on your investment worthwhile?

The three elements of a successful salary agreement include:

1. Mutual respect
2. Gain for both parties
3. Strong foundation for a long-term, solid working relationship

Salary

At this point you should be aware of the candidate's present salary and he should be aware of the position's salary range. You've done your research and he's done his. This is where salary negotiations begin.

Several factors come into play that can help make your offer attractive and competitive. One key factor is current market value for comparable positions. Online resources, such as HR Salary Wizard, make it easy to ascertain a position's market value. Given the current economy though, while some candidates may be very open minded when it comes to salary, you want to think long term; you want the compensation package to be satisfying enough that when the economy improves, your employee will not seek employment elsewhere for more money.

Another thing to consider when determining the salary offer is the level of the position. Typically you have more bargaining room with higher level positions. That does not mean that there is not room for negotiation at a lower level position. You'll want to take several factors into account and consider your investment in the hiring process.

Factors to consider when determining salary offer:

- Candidate's present salary and salary expectation
- Position's salary range within your organization
- Position's level within your organization
- Fair market value of the position within the industry
- Level of the candidate's skills and experience
- Additional benefits within your corporate structure

Obviously, you will also need to consider how much time went into the process of identifying and interviewing the present candidate, how badly you need to fill the position, and how easily you can proceed to the next candidate if this one rejects your offer. You have likely made a big investment in time and resources to reach this point. You want to start building a long-term, mutually beneficial relationship, so weigh each factor carefully in determining the appropriate salary offer.

Benefits

Benefits vary from company to company but generally they can be as much as 35% of an individual's wages. As discussed in earlier chapters, there are many reasons a candidate would be motivated to make a career move, and your benefits package could be a determining factor in the ultimate decision.

This is where you can get creative. Especially if you do not have as much room to negotiate salary, as may be the case with small businesses, consider other financial inducements such as signing bonuses. Additionally, "lifestyle" benefits such as flextime and telecommuting options may provide further incentive. Does the candidate require flextime, for example, or is your company more family friendly than his present employer? These and other items in your benefits package could be enough to sway his decision above and beyond the salary you are offering.

These additional items of compensation may include:

- Health insurance
- Dental insurance
- Vision insurance
- Life insurance
- Retirement/Pension plans
- 401 (k) or 403(b) plans
- Flextime
- Vacation time
- Sick leave
- Maternity/Paternity/Family leave
- Compensatory time

- Holidays
- Education allowance
- Professional development
- Child Care
- Stock options
- Bonuses
- Car/phone/travel expenses
- Employee recognition

Just as the constituency of the workforce has changed over the years, the individual needs of employees have changed, and employers are finding it necessary to respond to these needs with various benefits packages. The more creative your company can be with a benefits package, the more attractive it will be to a perspective employee. And remember, not all incentives need to take the form of financial incentives.

Several years ago we had a candidate who stated his salary requirements, which we knew were unrealistic. Many times candidates state the amount they need or want instead of what the realistic industry standard is for the job. In this case the company offered benefits that were exceptional, including tuition reimbursement and a car allowance. Once we put down on paper how much these benefits were worth, the candidate reconsidered his salary requirements.

Personal considerations

It's all about the candidate!

While salary and benefits are certainly key factors affecting a candidate's decision to take a job, there are personal reasons that can be equally compelling. There could be a strained relationship or uncomfortable environment at the candidate's present company. He could be seeking an environment that is more family friendly, enabling him time to help care for a new baby or sick parent. He may require a more flexible schedule to work out daycare situations. Job location, commute time, ability to work from home, and other such personal factors all enter into the decision-making process, and what's most important will vary from candidate to candidate.

Again, from the candidate's perspective, what's in it for him is more important at the moment than what's in it for you and your company. Consider the complete package – salary, benefits, and any personal considerations you may be aware of – as objectively as possible from the point of view of the candidate and take this into account when making the offer.

Finally, don't underestimate the power of personal rapport. You are looking to build a long-term, mutually beneficial relationship. You and other members of your company who have been involved in the interview process will likely have positive feelings toward your top candidate, and, if everything went according to plan, he will have an equally positive perception of you and your company. This will also have an impact on his decision when contemplating your offer.

I know of one case in which the candidate's new position would require him to travel a lot. The hiring manager sent a gift basket to the candidate's spouse, essentially thanking her for her support. This cemented the relationship between the spouse and the hiring manager, and made the candidate feel good about his decision to take the new position.

The offer

When you are prepared to make an offer, act quickly and make it verbally. Follow up immediately with a written offer including all the details. You want to demonstrate your professionalism as well as present the opportunities within your company. If you have planned a start date, allow adequate time for the candidate to resign graciously from his present employment. The interview process is not simply about selecting the best candidate, but ensuring that the best candidate selects you as well.

I advise it's best to make your best offer up front and let the candidate know it is your best offer. Discuss how susceptible the candidate is to a counter offer from his company. It's important to know what is inspiring him to make a move, and how inclined he would be to think about the counter offer.

This is also a good reason to have several top candidates in mind rather than just one. If a candidate were to receive a counter offer, you could let him know you have several others under consideration for the position which may deter him from thinking about the counter offer too seriously, and, should he accept the counter offer, you are not left starting your search over.

The offer letter

I have been an expert witness twice in court, both times relating to offer letters. A weak offer letter that does not include the necessary components, no matter how well intended, can open the company up for a lawsuit.

While an offer letter may seem like a formality, it can be considered an employment contract, and therefore should be given careful attention. Putting the specifics in writing delineates responsibilities, shows the importance of the position and demonstrates how valued the individual you are hiring is.

I've seen cases where the offer was not put in writing, and the situation ends up in court because of miscommunication, misinterpretation of facts and assumptions. I saw one case in which the client did an "engagement letter" rather than an offer letter, but I would advise that this is too vague and it is always best to write a thorough offer letter.

In the case of this "engagement letter," it covered the basics, but it was missing some key components and it was subject to interpretation. The candidate's expectations were not met and the client's expectations were not clearly delineated as to what was compensation, and it resulted in a nasty lawsuit.

The offer letter serves to record the new employment relationship. It should accurately document the employer's expectations, as well as obligations. Because there are several things you'll want to clearly define, the letter can come across as formal. You can lessen this by using simple, direct language and welcoming messages in both the opening and closing of the letter.

Components of an effective offer letter include:

1. Position and reporting structure
2. Responsibilities
3. Nature of employment (at-will or for a term)
4. Compensation (Complete package including salary, benefits, bonuses, stock options, etcetera)
5. Non-compete/non-disclosure agreements
6. Condition that employee will confirm in writing that employment does not conflict with any present/former employment agreements
7. Expiration date for offer

A good offer letter should clearly define the position and reporting structure so there is no question as to the expectations by both parties. You should also indicate however, that these are subject to change as business needs evolve. Unless there is a specific term of employment, a simple "at-will statement" should also be included, indicating that the employee is employed "at-will" and both parties can terminate employment at any time, with or without notice, reason or cause.

Clearly define the compensation package in your offer letter, including base salary, benefits and any bonuses or equity. In the case of bonuses, be specific as to whether the employee will receive a set amount or "up to" an amount based on predetermined parameters. If bonuses are performance based, be clear about specific targets that must be met in order to receive the bonus. You should also make it understood that a bonus is discretionary based on employee performance as determined by management, if that is the case. Any equity compensation such as stock options should also be plainly delineated in the offer letter.

The offer letter should also include any non-compete or non-disclosure statements required by your company. Any such agreements requiring signatures are also best included with the offer letter, thereby reducing the potential for a new employee to say he was misled into accepting the position and asked to sign restrictive covenants after the fact.

By the same token, you will likely want to protect your company from any employment agreement the candidate has with the current or former employer. This is easily handled by having the candidate confirm in writing that he has no agreements with present or former employers that would preclude his employment with your company.

You may also want to include an expiration date for the offer. This will ensure the position does not remain open for an extended, indeterminate period of time.

Countering the counter offer

As mentioned previously, you may find that once your top candidate attempts to resign from his present position, he receives a counter offer from his current employer. You may consider this a negative obstacle to your goal of hiring the candidate, but in fact it may be a positive turn of events.

Many recruiters would counsel a candidate to hesitate on the current employer's counter offer. For the most part, top performers looking to make a move are motivated by more than money. If the current employer is suddenly willing to come through with more money or a promotion, why wasn't it presented before the resignation? The candidate should consider that he was undervalued or taken for granted, and once the current employer gets what he wants – the candidate to remain in his present position – he is likely to return to his old ways.

What's more, for most top performers looking to make a move, the motivation is more than money. It goes back to the career wound referenced earlier. It may be a strained relationship, poor management, a perception of company instability, change in responsibility or some other issue, but these cannot be overcome with a salary increase or title change. These negative issues will continue to be present at the current employer, and will have a decided impact on the candidate's consideration of the counter offer.

The positive for you as the perspective employer is that if the present employer is working to keep him, clearly you have hit upon a valuable candidate. You are seeing some recognition of his worth as an employee and confirmation of your estimation of him.

At this point then, you need to consider how much room you have to negotiate further to show your commitment to this candidate. Since his motivation is likely larger than money, a small increase in salary may be appropriate, or you may choose to offer a signing bonus. The advantage of the signing bonus is that it is a one-time expense for you.

In some cases no increase may be appropriate. Perhaps you have made your best offer and you feel strongly about it being a good, fair offer. Again, consider your total offer package in your contemplation of any counter, counter offer. Don't be afraid to point out the advantages your company is offering over the candidate's present employer. Remind him of what you value in him as a perspective employee and of the opportunity your position and your company offer him. Reaffirm that your position complements his talent, life and lifestyle. This can be the perfect opportunity to make the candidate feel good about coming to work for your company.

When to move on

Not every candidate will jump at every offer. If there is hesitation or a counter offer, consider the source of the indecision. If it's a matter of a greater salary, you have to decide whether or not it promises an adequate return on your investment. If there are personal considerations, will the outcome of hiring this candidate prove mutually beneficial in the long run depending on those considerations? Weigh your options and take into account the reservations, and know when it's best to move on to the next candidate.

Chapter 7:
Onboarding: Accommodate, acclimate, accelerate new members to the team

Your ideal candidate has accepted your offer and is ready to begin work with your company. You want to welcome him, orient him and give him a foundation for success. However, you'd like him to "hit the ground running," and so he may. However, taking a holistic approach to the honeymoon period is worth the time and effort, because while it encompasses welcoming and orienting a new employee, onboarding is more about retention and forging that long-term relationship than orientation.

The 3 A's of Onboarding

Accommodate your new employee. This stage is all about reducing any new employee anxiety. It is where you are reaching out, welcoming him to the company and providing the basic tools from telephone, computer, access information, orientation and contact with colleagues so the employee feels comfortable and at ease in his new environment.

Accentuate the positive. This is the next level of business: providing the training and guidance necessary to succeed in the position. This is where you make sure the new employee understands the job and related expectations. It is also where he should feel more fully acclimated into the corporate culture as you encourage socialization and foster a sense of belonging.

Accelerate to productivity. This phase involves establishing priorities and giving and taking feedback. This is where you can make appropriate adjustments and improvements in your new employee's performance as well as your onboarding process so that everything is moving forward in a mutually beneficial manner.

If orientation introduces the path to success, onboarding is the highway, the road *best* travelled. You want to attract the new employee, confirm his interest and help him become accustomed to his new company where he will feel like an integrated part of the team. This road is a two-way street: the new employee is making an effort to get up to speed on the company, contribute and produce, and you are learning more about his aspirations and motivations, involving and challenging him in ways that are meaningful and important to him so he can remain content and productive.

That's why an effective onboarding process will have an impact on employee engagement. The Human Resources Corporate Leadership Council "found that increasing an employee's level of engagement could potentially improve performance by 20 percent and reduce the employee's probability of departure by a whopping 87 percent!"[2]

Internal resources, social media and software and technology will help you introduce the employee to new systems and a new corporate culture, values and the 'norms' of your company. These tools will also help you monitor his ease of connecting to his new environment.

There are three goals of bringing a new employee "on board":

1. Welcome the new employee and make him feel comfortable as part of the team
2. Minimize the employee's time to productivity
3. Establish a foundation for long-term success and a mutually

---

[2]   Silkroad Technology, Creating an Onboarcing Process 2010

beneficial relationship

Many companies are now automating much of their onboarding programs in order to maximize efficiency. Electronic forms, task management and portals are designed to quickly assimilate employees into the company culture. This is valid and practical, but it's important to maintain the human element involved in the onboarding process. One of your goals is to help the employee feel comfortable in his new environment. Interaction with team members and other department employees will be very important as well.

Set specific objectives for your onboarding process. Determine when certain proficiencies should be met along the new employee's path and coordinate the program appropriately. Maintain a steady pace to ensure retention of the skills and knowledge achieved along the way. Ultimately, it is your company that will enjoy the benefits of an effective onboarding process.

I usually don't mention client names but I'm going to in this instance. Of all the clients I've worked with – and I've worked with hundreds – By Appointment Only (BAO) has, by far, the strongest onboarding program I've ever seen. The vice president of human resources and the staff provide an extraordinary onboarding process that is solid, strong and consistent. Candidates feel like they're part of the team before they even step foot in the door. Many of the aspects that BAO incorporates into their onboarding process are included in this chapter.

Set goals

One of the things to consider in your onboarding program is specific objectives. What is the duration of the program? What impressions do you want the employee to come away with? What are the measurable skill sets and body of knowledge you want the employee to achieve?

Determine a timeline with action items, including who is responsible for each action. Decide which people are involved, including human resources, senior management, managers, supervisors as well as co-workers.

Define all expectations at the onset of the program so the employee has a clear understanding of what it takes to be successful. This also enables the employee to take ownership by recognizing his goals within the company and acquiring the tools to accomplish those goals. Establish goals for 30 days, 90 days and even as far as six months and one year.

You can arrange an in-person survey or include an online survey on your Intranet with different questions for each stage of the onboarding process. Early questions might focus on the welcoming process, the first day and whether there are any concerns with technology such as computers, phones, etc. Follow in the next intervals with questions relating to the tools, skills and body of knowledge you are trying to impart to the new employee to determine if he is successfully acquiring these. Finally you may want to ask about his own strategic goals once he has been involved in the onboarding process for some time.

Evaluating the employee's progress at specified intervals can help determine where more effort is needed, both on the company's part in providing the necessary information and tools to do the job, as well as on the employee's part in attaining maximum productivity. If something is lacking, you can modify your program to make the most of the onboarding process.

Reach out

The onboarding process should begin even before the new hire has his foot in the door. Reach out and get as much accomplished before the actual start date as is practical. Certainly all paperwork should be in place.

Hiring document checklist

- Completed, signed application
- Signed release to contact references
- Immigration Reform and Control Act (IRCA) documents
- Fair Credit Reporting Act (FCRA) disclosures/concent
- Signed offer letter
- Signed non-disclosure/non-compete agreements
- Signed copy of sexual harassment policy
- Signed receipt of company handbook
- Signed receipt of any key company policies
- COBRA rights notice

Equally important is helping the new employee feel welcome before he reports to work. Be sure he knows the basics: where to go on the first day, whom to ask for on arrival, appropriate attire, starting time, normal business hours, etcetera. Call and ask if he has any additional questions that you can answer or if there are any special considerations for that first day. You may also want to provide early access to the company Intranet.

The first day can sometimes be a little laborious with extensive information and abundant introductions. Try to achieve a comfortable balance between instruction and levity, allowing for some less formal meetings and down time.

Orient

To some extent, the onboarding process begins during the interview stage. It is there where you introduce your corporate culture and begin to define your company values. This segment of the process will continue during an orientation program.

The orientation provides a useful overview of the company, departments, goals and objectives. Start with the basics. Be sure your new employee has everything he needs upon arrival: a computer or laptop with all the necessary software, a company email address and account, and adequate office supplies. A mug, notepad or pen with the company logo can go a long way in making the employee feel quickly at home. After some initial introductions, you'll want to begin the orientation.

A typical orientation program includes:

- Housekeeping items
- Policies and procedures
- Company/departmental overview
- Job expectations

This portion of the onboarding program involves a range of people at your company from human resources representatives, to department supervisor and possibly even coworkers who will all work together to help integrate your new employee into the company.

Housekeeping items include all the little details a new employee will need to know but may not even think to ask. These items include normal work hours, overtime pay, dress code, inclement weather procedures, contact numbers, etc.

Policies and procedures are more formal and include things like equal opportunity employment, hostile work environment, sexual harassment, and outside employment policies. Employee compensation guidelines, time and attendance reporting, vacation and holidays, sick leave, grievance procedures and any other company policies are included here. These items are often provided in an employee handbook and are presented by human resource staff.

While much of this material may be dull, it is important to be thorough and clearly define all necessary policies and procedures in order to ensure a smooth transition of the new hire into effective employee. If there are several new employees, a group orientation that enables the new people to interact can be very efficient and effective in putting them further at ease.

While your new hire received some idea of the company's overall mission and values during the interview stage, these are more clearly spelled out in the onboarding program. Provide a thorough vision of both the department and the company, along with organization charts, in order to illustrate how all areas of the team contribute. This information will help the new employee understand his role as well as the department's role in helping to meet the company goals.

Job expectations will also be familiar to the new employee from the interview stage where they would have already been clearly defined. It is important to elaborate on them again during onboarding so that there is no confusion later on. Review the duties of the job, expectations and performance appraisal system. With a clear picture of the job expectations and performance management, the employee will know what it takes to be successful in the new position.

Consider scheduling a lunch during the first day of orientation so that the new employee can meet and interact with coworkers. It can be helpful to have representatives from different departments throughout the company join the lunch. It is also a good idea to have the employee's supervisor and mentor attend. You may want to schedule these types of meet and greet lunches throughout the first week to help the new employee get to know his coworkers and feel comfortable in his new environment.

Automate

Software and online packages are available to help streamline onboarding. These automated products offer efficiency and ease the routine aspects involved in the process. Automating form delivery helps ensure the new employee doesn't spend the first day filling out redundant paperwork. You can schedule workflow using automatic task-triggers and reminders. You can provide access to training and human resource materials as well as enable the new employee to stay connected to other employees.

Many automated programs enable you to coordinate between the many departments involved in your onboarding program, including Human Resources, IT, managers, facilities and other parts of your organization. You can also conduct surveys to obtain feedback about your onboarding process.

The benefits of automating include less paperwork, increased efficiency, reduced costs and a full audit trail if needed. At the same time it aids the new employee in feeling prepared and connected in his new position.

Training

Where orientation offers a helpful overview, training provides the nuts and bolts of what is necessary for success in the position and the organization. Some companies may have a complete training manual online. This can be a helpful resource, but may not be solely effective at engaging a new employee.

It takes time for a new employee to familiarize himself with your product or service, market and competition. Providing adequate training is another way to help accelerate your new employee to productivity. As with the other elements involved in the onboarding program, this not only helps aid in productivity, but furthers retention by helping the employee feel comfortable and well equipped to accomplish the job. Consider training as an investment in both your employee and your company, rather than a cost.

Determine what areas or skills will best address your company's current and future needs. Sales training, for example, may focus on communication skills, sales tools, strategies, as well as knowledge of the product or industry. Effective sales training programs can provide your salespeople with the tools to achieve measurable performance goals and give your company a competitive edge.

Be sure that you have the right training materials and instructors to effectively communicate during the training process. Where you conduct training is also important. If you're using a training room, be sure it is a comfortable environment conducive to learning outfitted with any necessary equipment. Work on engaging employees during training so they will better retain the information. In addition, it is often effective to follow up several weeks later with reinforcement training.

Organized, ongoing training is an important investment in your employees and therefore your company, and should not be limited to new hires. You can show your team the value of professional development and demonstrate your commitment to helping all members of the team succeed with a strong, ongoing training program. You'll not only strengthen their individual skills, you'll help motivate them to continually improve and grow professionally and within your organization.

Mentoring

Mentoring is extremely beneficial in the onboarding and training process. Assign a seasoned employee to address questions and concerns, as well as show the ropes to the new employee. This relationship can play a key role in integrating the new employee into the corporate culture, making him feel connected and comfortable, and helping him achieve success.

Not only does a strong onboarding program help retain valued employees, but studies show that mentoring in combination with onboarding has a substantial impact on employee retention.

Mentoring encourages an individual who is experienced to share his knowledge. It gives him a sense of added responsibility and sometimes accountability to help the new employee.

In addition to a body of knowledge the mentor conveys to the new employee, to some extent the mentor can also evaluate how the individual is acclimating into his new environment and fitting into the corporate culture. The mentor can assess how the new employee is absorbing the information and whether or not he is learning at an acceptable rate. If not, the mentor can help the department or supervisor make any necessary adjustments.

New employees who have a mentor tend to transition into corporate culture faster and be up and running faster. They come to respect those with more experience instead of viewing them as adversaries. At the same time the mentor passes on his knowledge, he becomes sharper because he knows someone else is watching.

It is not an expensive proposition to establish a mentoring program. Most can be based on a small compensation, bonus or other compensation such as acknowledgment, title or recognition in front of peers.

Successful mentor qualities:

- Desire to serve as mentor
- In-depth body of knowledge about the company, its product/service, market and industry
- Clear understanding of and accord with corporate culture and values
- Effective communication skills

- Respected by peers, management
- Successful in position
- Accepts responsibility for failures and is open to sharing them with new employee

The use of mentors further demonstrates the company's commitment to its employees. It shows that the company values the new employee by investing the time of the mentor in his training and acclimation. It also shows that the company values the mentor himself as a representative of the company and its values.

Honeymoon period

The honeymoon period is the first three months of employment when the employee is taking the opportunity to settle into his new position. During the early stages the employee is getting to know his coworkers, new environment and company procedures and policies. Soon after, the settling-in phase begins in which the employee begins to take on responsibility and establish his routine.

It is important that he be able to clearly identify management's priorities and expectations and establish solid working relationships within the company. It is also important to help him embrace the corporate culture, including any technology that is new to him.

Mentoring can play a key role during this period of employment. The mentor will introduce the employee to coworkers, help him assimilate into the corporate culture, check to be sure he's comfortable with all the appropriate technology, and convey a sense of what it takes to be successful within the company.

During the honeymoon period the employee tends to have a heightened sense of enthusiasm and fulfillment regarding the position because he is full of expectations. He is focused on making a good impression with his new employer and wants to convey a positive attitude, which helps to generate a period of intense satisfaction.

By six months the initial enthusiasm has generally worn off and settles into a more realistic sense of satisfaction. During this time when job satisfaction may be depleting to some extent, it can be helpful to engage the employee and provide added support if needed. Offer additional opportunities, if possible, and work to ensure the employee feels connected and valued.

These cycles of extreme satisfaction and depletion of the intensity of satisfaction are normal in the first six months of employment. Understanding this should make it easier to manage and help maintain the productivity and effectiveness of your onboarding program. You are working to build that long-term relationship with your employee and your complete onboarding process will establish a firm foundation for that mutually successful relationship.

Give and take

While you're busy trying to make the new hire feel at home, providing the necessary tools to succeed, and demonstrating his value to the company, your new hire should be doing his part. He should be proactively learning everything he can about your company, products and corporate culture, and asking appropriate questions along the way. These questions can communicate a lot about his level of interest, aptitude and potential for productivity. Pay attention. Take the opportunities presented by a question or observation on the part of the new employee to offer guidance and feedback.

In fact, feedback should be an important component of your onboarding program. Consider adding performance appraisals several times within the first year. These enable the new hire to see how he's doing and make adjustments before an annual review. Periodic appraisals also provide you with more structured opportunities to offer guidance and direction where necessary.

Identifying missteps and guiding forward

You're investing time and money in your onboarding program so you will want to be able to measure its impact. One-on-one interviews, focus groups and surveys are some tools you can use to help determine the success of your program. Some questions that may be useful include:

- Did you feel welcomed?
- Did you have a telephone/telephone number, computer, access information, etc. on your first day?
- Was your manager involved in the onboarding process?
- Were the job expectations and goals clearly spelled out?
- Did you have the tools and resources needed to do your job?
- How satisfied were you with the onboarding program overall?
- What suggestions to you have to improve the program?

Questions will vary depending on when and how often you choose to evaluate the program.

You may find that there are some missteps on the part of your new employee even with your most careful planning, onboarding and nurturing. It is important to look at the mistake from an objective viewpoint and evaluate where the company can improve its training, onboarding and communication of information with the employee so that the misstep does not happen again.

Determine what strategic concerns may have led to the problem. Step back and avoid reacting emotionally by reprimanding the employee, the supervisor or the hiring manager. Find the root cause of the misstep, see what steps can be taken to correct it going forward and avoid it in the future, and communicate with the employee.

Take these opportunities to learn from mistakes, cultivating your relationship with the individual through one-on-one discussions about what went wrong, how to address the misstep and how to avoid it in the future. This will help him learn from the mistake and help maintain his comfort level within his new position.

An employee mentor can be helpful during this process. Hopefully the new hire will have a strong relationship with the mentor by the time any error occurs, so he will be able to take constructive feedback and continue to benefit from the mentoring relationship in more troublesome circumstances.

Onboarding is an important means of engaging the new employee and transitioning him to be a productive member of the team. An investment in a comprehensive, systematic onboarding program is ultimately an investment in your company.

Chapter 8:

Retention: Keep Your Best at Their Best

In today's world, tenure is not what it was. Back in the late '80s and early '90s when companies were going through an economic downturn, they took the viewpoint that they could no longer be paternalistic.

401Ks, for example, came out of this thinking. Instead of a pre-defined pension provided by the company, employees were asked to contribute to their retirement savings, taking a more active role. Where there future would have at one time been provided for by the company, the employees were left to take control and plan for themselves.

Fast forward 30 years, and you now have a generation in the workforce that understands the need to be self-oriented. An individual no longer expects to be with one company until retirement. He or she will stay with a company as long as the company continues to challenge him or her, provide financial stability, enrichment, development, etc. When the company no longer fulfills that role, they will look for another company to meet his needs.

Morale and motivation: Engaging the workforce

So how do you tap into what motivates your best people to keep them as long as you can? There is no great secret to motivating people. Keeping up the morale of your workforce and inspiring your team members to perform at their best is simply a matter of TRUST.

T alent

R ecognition & reward

U pward growth

S atisfaction

T rust

You appreciate the value of good people. You've invested a great deal in attracting and attaining top talent. You know that the individuals who make up your workforce are the backbone of your company. This is the basis for successful retention. Start with the right people and have them in the right places.

The next step is to convey that appreciation to the individuals who make up the team. It is important that they feel valued. We'll get into this further in the next section of this chapter, but it is important that the company effectively implement a recognition program and reward top performers to encourage continued job satisfaction and productivity.

In keeping with this, it is critical to constantly engage the members of your team. Recognize their accomplishments. Listen to their ideas. Work with them to learn from failures and build on successes. As much as possible, allow them to be involved in decision-making.

While much of this should be face to face, you can make use of your company Intranet as well as the forums of social media. Quality people want to contribute to the team and want to feel that their contribution is valued.

The rules of employee engagement are simple:

Communicate. Relay appropriate information regarding the employee's position, performance and prospects. Solicit his feedback and input. Listen when he makes suggestions. Employees who feel they are able to offer suggestions and have consequential conversations with superiors are more apt to contribute because they feel valued.

Clarity of company goals and ongoing communication are important factors in employee engagement. Employees who understand the company's goals, how their role impacts the team and those goals, and how the company appraises employees based on realization of those goals tend to be more engaged and more committed to the organization. Open, two-way communication is paramount.

Innovate. Be creative in your approach to engaging your employees. Know what motivates them and find ways to tap into and augment that motivation. Develop new ways to blend the personal and professional priorities of your team. Invest in new technology, equipment and resources when suitable.

Be very supportive of your employees' side pursuits and outside activities. This motivates them to work. Whether charitable work or their children's activities, devise ways to show your support. A day off every six months for a charitable effort or corporate matching for charitable contributions, for instance, can go a long way toward building loyalty.

Enable. Provide the tools, resources, and leadership necessary to succeed in the job. Offer career development and advancement opportunities. Ensure a corporate culture that nurtures, develops, recognizes and rewards talent. Encourage and reward creativity. Innovative training and a culture of training and constant improvement helps you to recruit and retain productive employees.

I had a client in the software industry in which competition for candidates was fierce. Compensation- and benefits-wise, my client couldn't match the packages of other companies. What did distinguish them was the way that they really enabled their employees.

They brought in various trainers for public speaking, new technology, etc.

They further supported charities of the employees, and went so far as to develop a committee to allocate funds for these charities. The employees were engaged in that they had a say in how the funds were disbursed. They were judicious about that responsibility. At the same time, the company could not be blamed if a particular organization did not get funds since it was the committee that made the determination. It was a win-win type of engagement for both the employees and the company.

One area where engagement can be especially useful is in addressing the needs and working relationships of various generations. Today's workforce is more diversified than ever. In addition to differing sex and ethnicity, generations as varied as Vets, Baby Boomers, Generation Xs, Generation Ys and Millennials all make up the same workforce in the same workplace, and the differences among work ethics and routines can be challenging.

Engage these employees. Help them understand the differences among the various generations and establish effective communication among different groups. Provide the forum for them to share knowledge, learn from each other and understand each other's contributions to the company. Each generation has unique characteristics and insights. Help your team appreciate the values that each member brings to the group.

I have found that while the older generation can offer the invaluable advantages of experience and life lessons, the younger generations are quite adaptable, willing to work when the work needs to be done, not just during traditional business hours. Both contributions are significant. Work with each segment of your workforce as a team, help them work together, and help them appreciate the contributions each has to offer.

In addition, the older generations can often serve as mentors to younger employees, offering the wisdom and knowledge they have acquired through the years. As the workforce ages as more and more people postpone retirement, companies should implement a plan to transfer the skills, knowledge and insight that the aging workforce population has to offer to the younger generations.

Older workers may not be as concerned about advancement opportunities and may be less prone to compete for promotions. Rather, they may be more motivated by the opportunity to feel that they are contributing something, such as mentoring a younger coworker. Older employees also tend to be more loyal, call out sick less, and stay with a company longer.

When dealing with various generations, take the time to consider what each brings to the table. Keep in mind that their motivations, drive and ideas about recognition and reward can vary greatly.

Again, there are many ways to engage employees at all levels. Team building opportunities, focus groups, luncheons, corporate Intranet, and social media are some effective means of connecting with your team and building momentum. Additional ideas to help you engage your workforce and develop a sense of community among your employees include:

- Suggestion box/forum
- Dress-down Friday
- Slogan/idea contests
- Periodic prize auctions
- Company picnics/holiday party
- Corporate newsletter

A key area involved in motivating and engaging your workforce is upward growth. Most people do not want to feel as if they are stagnating. By and large people want to know that they are advancing, always learning and progressing. Top performers will not settle for a lack of career growth.

Ongoing training and career development will go a long way in engaging your employees and motivating them to continually improve, thus improving productivity. Encouraging continual career development and growth shows the employee that you value him, and that you're willing to continue investing in him. Challenge your employees and provide opportunities for them to take on greater responsibility in order to prime them for future advancement.

Provide opportunity by highlighting your talent mobility program. Talent mobility draws from your existing pool of employees to fill open positions within your company. There are four major benefits to implementing a talent mobility program:

1. Reduced talent acquisition costs
2. Reduced turnover
3. Reduced ramp-up time
4. Increased employee engagement

In fact, internal opportunities and career development can be foremost factors involved in employee engagement. Make the most of your employees by enabling them to make the most of your upward growth opportunities. Even lateral promotions may be viewed as opportunities to learn and add new skills to the employee's work experience.

Each of these factors, recognition, reward, engagement and growth opportunities, contribute to the employee's job satisfaction. Job satisfaction is a shared commitment in which the employee is committed to learning, contributing and producing, and you inspire loyalty and a sense of fulfillment for his positive efforts and results. Studies indicate that when an employee experiences job satisfaction he is more likely to be effective and productive. A positive work culture is established by you and reinforced by your employees.

This goes hand-in-hand with the mutual trust and respect necessary to build morale and motivate your people. When the employee feels he has the respect of the company and his superiors, he works to live up to that sense of worth. When the company is functioning optimally with top talent in place, operational efficiency, an engaged workforce, and effective recognition and rewards, the employee returns that respect for the company as well, reflecting it in his performance.

This foundation of TRUST in the morale and motivation of your workforce is a cyclical process. Each segment builds upon the one before it, creating a positive working environment where each team member's fundamental motivators are met, and the team member contributes in turn. The result is continuous productivity and growth for your company.

Recognition and rewards

Employee recognition can take so many forms it's hard to know where to begin. What's important to remember is a little recognition can be a big, big step toward employee job satisfaction and continued performance. It's also important to offer both short- and long-term incentives. There needs to be some sense of immediate gratification for the employee as well as goals to work toward.

An effective recognition program reinforces the behaviors and attitudes you want to encourage in your employees. Your program should be open to all employees, should include specific criteria for earning recognition, and the recognition should occur as close to the accomplishment being recognized as possible. For little or no cost, you can boost morale and engage your workforce.

Examples of employee recognition:

- Employee of the month wall photo or reserved parking space //
- Top sales person of the month wall photo or reserved parking space
- Recognition at meeting or event
- Mention in corporate newsletter
- Mention on Intranet site/social media sites
- Thank you letter from company
- Lunch on the company
- Years-of-service award
- Award certificate
- Promotional items with company logo
- Comp time
- Preferred parking space for successful referrals

One client I work with makes it a point to have a luncheon once a month for employees with an anniversary during that month. There is no agenda, just lunch. It's a means of recognizing the employees, but it also enables the employees to bond with each other because they find others in the company with whom they share an anniversary or something else in common. This is a great opportunity to both recognize and encourage bonding within your team.

Recognition is an investment in employee morale as well as your corporate culture. Many forms of recognition don't cost anything at all, but go a long way toward engaging and motivating your workforce. To make the most of your employee recognition program, keep it simple, keep it fair, and keep it consistent.

While the concept of rewards overlaps recognition, there is more of a monetary value associated with rewards. Rewards are in addition to salary and generally have some expense to the company. As with various forms of recognition, they are used to motivate employees and reward performance.

Financial rewards, such as bonuses, stock options and profit sharing, are tied to an employee's specific accomplishments as set forth upon employment, and therefore should not be confused as entitlements. An effective reward program must have a clear means of measurement in order to earn the reward and must be plainly communicated to the employee. Because the reward has a cost to the company, it should be tied to a direct benefit for the company or company goal.

Bonuses are one example of a reward based on performance and are often used to motivate sales people to meet specific objectives beyond their basic tasks. Again, these should be tied to specific business goals, such as higher profits or new business. They may be based on individual performance, or if the objective is team building, may be based on group performance.

Stock options, in which the employee is permitted to purchase a certain number of shares in the company at a fixed price for a specified amount of time, are becoming more widely used as a means of reward. Stock option programs generally reward people for staying with the company as they are available after a number of consecutive years of employment. The employee must be fully vested in order to purchase stock, and then has the right to keep or sell the shares on the open market.

A benefit of stock option programs to the company is the ability to take a tax deduction as a compensation expense when issuing shares to employees who exercise their options. In addition, current accounting practices do not require businesses to show options as an expense, thus inflating the company value.

However, there are some risks to both company and employee with stock options programs. If accounting rules were to change, the company's earnings could be affected. Also, when an employee exercises an option, the company must issue an option that can be publicly traded. The company's market capitalization increases with the price of the market share, not the strike price, the fixed price originally agreed to. There could be a reduction in company earnings if the company has more shares outstanding, so the earnings must increase at the same rate as the outstanding shares or the company would have to repurchase outstanding shares on the open market. For the employee, if the option's strike price is higher than the market price, the employee's option is of no value.

In profit sharing an employee earns a percentage of corporate profits, which are generally paid out after a company has closed its books for the year. The disbursements can be made either as cash or as contributions to the employee's 401(k) program. The 401(k) may be combined with a new comparability profit-sharing plan, which enables the company to provide enhanced benefits to select employees meeting specified criteria, thus rewarding top performers. The profit-sharing type of reward enables companies to keep fixed costs low.

As with stock options, profit sharing also rewards employees for staying with the company because the program usually requires an employee to be vested over a specified number of years, rewarding employees for their contribution to the company's achieved profit goals.

To some extent, your total benefits package falls under recognition and rewards because it plays a role in retaining your top talent. In an increasingly competitive business environment, your benefits package both helps attract top performers as well as retain them by adding to job satisfaction. Health and dental insurance, paid time off, vacation days and other elements in your package all contribute to an employee's perception of how much the company values its employees.

Another means to reward a good employee that doesn't cost you anything: give him greater responsibility. Let them take ownership of a project or area under your authority or ask them to mentor a new team member. Step back and give them the freedom to exercise their own judgment and leadership. This can be especially constructive if advancement opportunities are limited due to budget constraints or downsizing, but be sure to publicly praise the employee appropriately and seek out advancement opportunities when possible.

Turning away turnover

Even in a positive, nurturing corporate culture, your competitors may try to woo your best employees. How do you put up barriers to discourage employees from considering outside offers?

While the standard non-compete and confidentiality agreements are a place to start, today's aggressive environment dictates that you take a more proactive approach. Be creative.

If most other companies are offering two weeks' vacation for the first five years of employment, offer three with five weeks' vacation at five years. Pay for a portion of membership at a local fitness center. Promote your training budget and host "lunch and learns." Bring in a financial advisor to provide free retirement and investment insight to employees.

Consider providing a "Financial Commitment Statement" which delineates the financial cost of everything the company provides to each employee: salary, social security, unemployment, disability, health care, vacation time, coffee, refreshments, whatever is applicable. Employees are often surprised to see the financial commitment a company makes to each employee. It is usually at least two times the employee's salary, and shows the value the company places on each employee.

Working hand-in-hand with a rewards and recognition program, your creative approach to combating turnover will provide a significant return on your investment.

Company self-evaluation: Top employee complaints

Retaining your top employees isn't hard if you know where to look for factors that would motivate them to leave: inward. In most cases what makes another opportunity more appealing is not necessarily more money or benefits, but rather that it's simply somewhere else. More often than not, dissatisfaction - whether with management, a supervisor, corporate values/culture, unrealistic sales quotas, or the company's perceived instability - is the primary reasons for turnover.

Therefore, it is imperative that you look inward and regularly assess your company, people, and environment to be sure all are contributing to keeping the backbone of your company at their best. To do so, start with the basics. Know what the typical complaints are, and evaluate to see how you measure up.

Some of the top employee complaints include:

Salary. Do you offer fair market value? Is there pay equity within your company? Are your salary increases the same for everyone, or based on merit and performance, rewarding merit and contribution?

Benefits package. Do you have a competitive benefits package, particularly in the areas of health and dental insurance?

Management. Do your managers empower their employees or micromanage? Is communication open? Are all employees treated fairly and equally? Do your employees feel supported? Is there favoritism or perceived signs of favoritism? Do the members of your management team lead by example? Do they demonstrate accountability?

Workload. Are employees spread too thin? Do they have the support they need to accomplish their tasks? Are there means to improve the flow of work? Are there means to voice suggestions for improvements? Does management have realistic objectives? Are sales quotas realistic?

Office environment. Do employees feel at ease in their surroundings? Do they have the equipment and materials they need to get the job done? Is the work space appealing and comfortable? Is the workplace free from prejudice, harassment and other issues that would make working there stressful? Is your Human Resource Department responsive to employee needs or seen as a pawn for the company?

If you find that any of these areas could be cause for concern, work with your team to find a solution. In some cases, a simple awareness of the issue will give rise to a plausible solution. In other instances, giving your employees a voice and enabling them to express their complaint or suggestion will alleviate some of their anxiety as long as they feel they are being taken seriously.

In the case of salary and benefits package, you need to determine what your company can afford in light of market value, industry standards and your bottom line. Objectively review whether you are being fair and equitable to all employees, while at the same time rewarding top performers for their contributions.

Many management issues can be resolved with proper training and communication about the planning, processes, and expectations of a given project or goal. Every member of the team should have a full understanding of the tasks at hand and his role in meeting the objectives.

Open communication is paramount. Employees need to feel encouraged to perform to the best of their abilities. If they experience any frustrations, they must feel comfortable voicing them. Supervisors and management should be reviewed for their ability to develop their team and respond to their concerns. Retention is indicative of the level of feedback to which you respond. An open dialogue between management and employees will help reduce turnover.

The ability to voice concerns is applicable to most situations, as in the case of workload, but employees should be encouraged to suggest solutions or improvements as well. Empower them to ask themselves, "How can I be part of a solution to this problem? How can I help make things better?" A suggestion box or recognition for good suggestions may help motivate employees to solve some of their own problems, while at the same time experience the satisfaction of management listening to their concerns.

The same is also true for office environment. If there is any area of uneasiness or anxiety, the employee needs to feel comfortable approaching management about it. Human Resources should play a major role in addressing interpersonal or any harassment issues, and must be seen as responsive and equitable in the resolution of these issues.

At the same time, do not simply consider Human Resources to be the policy police. They should be a strategic partner in understanding and supporting corporate culture. Be sure to provide them with the information and insights needed to present your company in a good light and promote a positive and productive environment.

Consider employee surveys and luncheon focus groups to help you take stock and learn where improvements can be made. Ask questions like: How did you come to this company? What makes you choose to stay? What do you know now that you wish you learned during the interview? Do you have any concerns that put you into a position where you feel you are not realizing your potential or getting the fullest extent of your opportunities?

Take the opportunity to learn from any missteps that you find. Evaluate why the misstep occurred and apply this to other situations within your company.

If you're getting positive feedback, ask for referrals! If your employee is happy and productive with your company, he may know someone who would also work well in the environment. Don't forget to reward the employee for the referral if a new employee comes on board and stays for six months or so.

I had the opportunity once of interviewing a candidate who was referred by someone who had left the company three weeks earlier for a position that was too phenomenal to pass up. I thought it was interesting that he referred his own replacement. He was not unhappy with the company he was leaving; he simply left for an opportunity that suited him better personally. Who better to know who could be successful in his former position than him, and we correctly anticipated that the referred candidate would do extremely well in the position.

Also, look at your top performers. Ask them if they have any areas of concern or suggestions for improvements. Learn from them.

Your team and its individual members are your most valuable assets. How you work beside them, communicate with them, recognize and reward them all works to nurture a mutual respect and trust necessary for a productive long-term, working relationship. If the worth you place on your employees is adequately communicated to them and reflected in your corporate values, turnover will be minimal.

Creating a corporate culture that demonstrates the value you place on your employees entails mindfulness and a simple understanding of human nature. With the right leadership, innovation and communication, you can foster a work environment that inspires loyalty, passion, problem solving and productivity.

Chapter 9:

Regrouping: When Good Decisions Go Bad

Don't be too quick to accept a hire that doesn't work out as part of the process and prepare to start over. This is a huge waste of your time, money and resources. Although a failed hire isn't out of the question, it should be an unlikely possibility if you've taken your time at each stage of the hiring process. At this point, take a step back, take a good, objective look at your efforts throughout the process, and determine where you went awry. Even in the case of a positive hire, do an autopsy after the position is filled to see where you can tweak your search and hiring process.

One of the downfalls of the information age is that there is enough information out there for some people to study and become excellent interviewees rather than truly excellent candidates.

One client told me a story about a candidate they hired who had presented herself well and answered all the questions in the interviews with enthusiasm and clarity. Everyone who had met with her was looking forward to her joining the team. When she started the job two weeks later she showed no enthusiasm and no clarity to the point that the team members were asking each other "Who is she?" When she was let go a short time later and asked where she thought the company went wrong in the hiring process, she said, "You all asked me the same questions and when I saw which answers worked best, I just kept giving those answers." After that, the company decided to invest in some training as to how to conduct interviews.

Identifying what went wrong to avoid it in the future

Start at the beginning. Does your job description convey the key responsibilities as well as goals and objectives of the position, or is it simply a laundry list of experience and skills you hope to see? Be sure your job description is up-to-date, clear, and accurately defines the role you seek to fill. Rather than describe the person you think could do the job, the job description should define success in the position.

Did you exhaust the pool of qualified candidates, or did you simply make your open position available to those actively seeking employment? As I've stated before, often the best people are not necessarily *looking* for a new opportunity, but may prove *open* to the right one if it is brought to their attention. Extensive networking should reach well beyond the job boards, web postings and social media to the top performers in the industry. Recruiters are in a unique position to reach these key players and are often the best resource to use when seeking qualified candidates.

Did the right people conduct the interview? Did the questions asked determine if the candidate had the ability to deliver the level of success as noted in the job description? Did the interviewers listen to the answers, taking notes when necessary, or did they spend more time talking about the company and position?

The interview questions need to be pointed enough to elicit insight into the candidate's personality and aptitude for the job in addition to his experience. They should be specific to the actual role he will be playing for your company.

Those people involved in the interview process need to take an objective look at their own objectivity. Did they remain impartial throughout the process or did they become emotionally invested on some level and let that sway their assessment of the candidate?

Were there adequate reference and background checks? Was the resume truly reflective of the candidate's background or were there details that were embellished? Again, due to legal ramifications involved in references, recruiters are often in a better position to provide a thorough reference check as they are most familiar with the industry and the key players on both ends – those who are top performers as well as those who employ them. In any event, be diligent about your reference checks as these can help predict a candidate's success.

Did you rush to fill the position? This sense of urgency can often distort your view of the candidate as well as aspects involved in the process itself. Take the time to attract the right candidates for the job, diligently screen the appropriate applicants and select the best fit for your needs.

Were expectations and performance measures clearly communicated? A lack of understanding of these elements can lead to motivation and engagement issues. While subjective factors such as cooperative attitude and drive are valid aspects of employee evaluation, take an objective look at the leadership involved with the employee to be certain ineffective communication is not a contributing factor.

Hiring Process Evaluation checklist:

1. Determine staff need
2. Job description
3. Recruitment plan
4. Search committee
5. Interview process
6. Evaluation process
7. Compensation package

8. Onboarding process
9. Employee engagement program

Look at the decision-making process

Decision making is a problem-solving activity that is complete once a suitable result has been determined. Your decision would involve a pre-determined set of criteria involving the job description, skill sets, experience and abilities, as well as less objective judgments based on interview and any additional communication throughout the process.

To some extent the decision is bound to be less than 100% rational; there is likely to be some emotional reaction along the hiring process that contributes to your ultimate decision. If you find that the person hired for the position is ultimately not the right fit, take a step back and evaluate your decision-making process throughout the overall process.

Many times the emotional element comes into play during the interview. Think back to your first meeting with the employee. Ask yourself how objective you were able to remain upon meeting the candidate and throughout the face-to-face interview. Were you able to postpone judgment and gather information regarding the candidate's accomplishments, or did you have a quick gut reaction that you sought to confirm? Were your questions consistent from interview to interview so that you had a basis for comparison among candidates? Were you subconsciously looking for someone in your own image?

Sometimes it's easy to assume the candidate you are interviewing will be great because you have something in common: you come from the same town or went to the same school, so you relate better. Someone once even told me they hired someone because she reminded him of his daughter. This is most often a mistake because you put less emphasis on the interview process and its objective components and more on the emotional aspects involved in human interaction.

One potential client once told me she was going to stop interviewing candidates because each time she recognized something in them that reminded her of herself, she would hire them. Then, of course, when they worked for her they would not react to situations the way she would and she would be disappointed.

As I've said throughout this book, the best interviewees are not necessarily the best candidates and vice versa. Your interview process should give you a good opportunity to determine and detect the qualities you are looking for in a candidate. When you find that doesn't happen and you've made a miss-hire, look back on the process and see if you've made some automatic, less-than-objective decisions on an individual. Did emotion come into play at some point and overrule objectivity?

Being objective and listening during an interview is the first step in making a good hire. A good rule of thumb is to look at the interview as a fact-finding mission and try to shelve your inclination to make a decision. Once you've collected a consistent core of information from all candidates you can collectively debrief with your team involved in the hiring process.

If you did debrief with your team, was it haphazard and disorganized, or was there a clear process in place for sharing information? Did some members of the team start with negative comments about any of the candidates that may have influenced the hiring team?

Consider implementing a procedure for sharing information that begins with the lowest-ranking members of your hiring team and starts with positive comments only. Once the positives have been shared, any negatives can then be communicated. It's okay to discuss "gut" feelings once all the appropriate data has been set forth and so long as it is not the sole deciding factor involved in your decision-making process.

Throughout your debriefing process, encourage differing points of view and make sure any "no" is justified with sound evidence. A "no" is certainly acceptable so long as it is based on facts and not emotional reactions.

If you struggled with the decision, consider implementing a three-point strategy for your decision making process.

1. Determine three or four primary competencies that the employee must have to be successful in the position.

2. Debrief with the team in a thorough, relaxed and fair manner. In the case of something as important as a new hire, more heads really are better than one.

3. Check the numbers. If you really are at a loss as to who is the best candidate, look at the assessment scores for any assessments you may have required and how these align with the job requirements. If you don't include assessments, consider adding them to your hiring process.

Preparing for the next hiring process

Whether you're planning to add to your staff due to corporate growth or replace an employee who hasn't worked out, your goal is to be prepared. Have a team evaluate your hiring process, assess your success as well as any failures, and determine where you can tweak the process to make improvements.

I had a client that hired four people in a sales class. Based on the interviews, one was very highly desirable and another was not expected to do extremely well. It turned out that first candidate ended up being a miss-hire. Although he'd interviewed well, upon further inspection it was determined that the interview process was superficial. It also turned out that the individual who did not interview as well worked out very well in the position.

After a miss-hire, go back and autopsy your process. Retune and realign the aspects of the interview process that are not giving you the perspective you need.

That particular client I just mentioned instituted a quantifying system we developed for the company. Retention went up 50 percent. We were able to reduce the amount of miss-hires by almost 30 percent. Take a look at your hiring process and then take a further look at your company.

Consider the environment. You can put an A player in a disconnected environment and you may see some temporary improvements, but you'll likely end up with long-term discontent and possibly turnover. Solicit feedback from other employees to determine if there are any environmental or engagement-related factors that may have influenced any malcontent leading to turnover.

Your hiring process should not be stagnant. You should constantly reevaluate and refine it to be sure it meets the needs of your evolving company. The job market changes, the economy changes, and your hiring process needs to adapt where necessary.

Your employees are the backbone of your company. Finding the right people for the right positions to keep your company at the forefront of your market should be an ongoing and evolving mission. It should not occur only in times of need. It is not stagnant. The time you spend evaluating, planning and improving your hiring process will likely produce substantial return on your investment in the long run.

Chapter 10:

When is it time to call a recruiter?

Some things are best left to an expert. I wouldn't suggest someone cut his own hair or perform his own heart surgery.

Even with my own taxes, I use TurboTax, but then hand everything over to my accountant. A few years ago my accountant found a $6,000 refund over a five-year period that TurboTax didn't know to look for. What I paid my accountant I got back more than 10-fold.

So when is it a good idea to turn to a recruiter who specializes in exactly that process which is key to your company's success? Here are several considerations:

1. You feel the need to broaden your search for qualified candidates, including those who may be happily at work producing for someone else.

2. Your current employees are feeling overworked and you're seeing a lack of productivity and, in turn, revenue.

3. You find yourself with applicants who are unprepared or are just not a good fit, wasting your valuable time.

4. You know where the good candidates are, but you're not comfortable calling your competitors and recruiting their employees out from under them.

The bottom line is you need to focus on running your business. The precious time it takes to go through a thorough recruiting process and due diligence on a candidate's background can best be spent working toward your company goals. The recruiting process can take as much as seven to 27 contacts with a candidate to complete, something a company simply doesn't have time for.

In fact, simmering – letting a candidate sit on the back burner with a watchful eye and occasional contact – can be a valuable means of building a pool of top talent to tap as the appropriate opportunities arise. It takes time, patience and perseverance.

This is one of several areas of expertise a recruiter brings to the table. A recruiter can take months or years to nurture relationships with the top players, build a rapport, and learn what key motivating factors may give rise to the perfect opportunity for both parties.

One of my most successful projects occurred when I had to identify candidates in a particular industry. Over a two-year period I spoke to 10 or so individuals in that industry who were considered strong candidates.

It took some time to convince my client that they could not force the issue. We identified the key candidates, but the client needed to be patient and wait for the candidate's availability. We did just that and my client was eventually able to get two of the top 10 key players in that industry during that two-year period because they adjusted their time schedule and waited until the candidates were ready to make a move at a time when it wasn't just about the money.

The client did not have to overpay. He was patient, kept the lines of communication open, and when the candidates were ready on their own terms, they did not interview anywhere else but with my client. By giving up control of the timeframe, the client gained control of securing the candidates best suited for the positions. This was a success for all concerned.

A good recruiter has the ability to develop a rapport and cultivate a relationship over the long term that can be used to a client's advantage when the time is right. What's more, the recruiter has a clear, comprehensive vision of the reality of the market: what the candidate pool is, what fair compensation is, what industry standards are, etcetera. An executive or manager in a company doesn't necessarily see this breadth of information on a regular basis, as a recruiter does, and may not be aware of the entire picture.

Even from the outset, when you post an ad, you will get candidates who are *reactive* to that stimulus. A recruiter can take a *proactive* role and readily determine which of those candidates are not viable. He can ask tougher questions during the interview stages that the company can't ask because of confidentiality issues. Undeniably, candidates are more likely to open up with a recruiter than a company interviewer.

Sourcing is an important area recruiters open up for clients. Sourcing is finding, discovering, uncovering, and identifying talented individuals to fill positions. If a client is doing his own sourcing he is likely to take the traditional route and place an ad in a newspaper, on job boards, on the company website, and maybe even on social media. But again, this only reaches a reactive audience – individuals who are reacting to seeing the ad. A good recruiter – and many recruiters are not good at sourcing – but a good recruiter can tap into that market that may not be actively searching, drawing on past relationships and reaching out to those who may not necessarily be looking for but would be open to a great opportunity.

What to look for

A strong recruiter is an expert in people study. He understands peoples' drives and motivations, and he's worked with enough to know how to find a good fit for all parties involved. The extent of a recruiter's experience and quality of reputation can tell you a lot.

A good recruiter should have:

- Ability to develop rapport
- Strong goal setting aptitude
- Clear vision to see the realities of the market, the company and the candidate
- Expertise on the market as well as client's individual needs
- Keen understanding of the competition in the market
- Appreciation for the client company's strengths and values as well as insight into any weaknesses
- Excellent communication
- Accessibility

When you are working with a recruiter, the recruiter should become a strategic partner focused on your long-term goals. He should not simply be looking to fill a present position, but rather to help build your company's future with a strong placement who will contribute to your bottom line and corporate growth over the long haul.

This partnership means some responsibility on your part as well. You must help the recruiter understand what your company's work environment is like, who the key executives are, what the company's core values are, and of course, what type of person you're looking for to compliment this environment. It is important that you help the recruiter understand what your company's unique selling power is and why someone would want to work for your company. Educate them on the way you do business so they can keep an eye out for talented individuals who can be strong additions to your team.

A good recruiter will be responsive to your needs, return phone calls promptly and not waste your time. How quickly you get back to a recruiter's questions reflects your company's sense of urgency and will be relayed back to the candidates. Again, you and the recruiter are working together in partnership to find the best possible candidate for your position.

Recruiter checklist

1. Years of experience
2. Credentials including professional certifications, designations and trade association memberships
3. Reputation, which may be based on industry references/placement history
4. Participation in industry events and conferences
5. Placement success rate
6. The 4 A's of a good recruiter

    Array - Levels of service offered

    Aptitude - Recruiting team resumes

    Accessibility - Communication commitment

    Accountability – Assuming responsibility

You may also want to inquire about the types of clients and industry experience, how candidates are screened and qualified, and whether or not they have an exclusivity policy which would prohibit you from working with other agencies.

I've had the privilege of working with many recruiters over the course of my career. Again, I don't usually name names, but I'd like to point out three exceptional recruiters who each have different styles and work with different companies.

Jeff Trail has had a wonderful career of helping companies expand and realign. He's been recruiting for more than 15 years and he has a very good ability to focus on clients.

Stu Goldblatt works frequently in the medical market. Over the last six years he's placed more than 60 people. What's interesting is that Stu really understands his clients' nuances and needs and is always thinking ahead. He works a lot with optometry companies. There are a limited number of candidates in this field, but Stu is able to take a proactive approach, building relationships with both candidates and clients to identify mutually beneficial arrangements.

Al Meyer is another exceptional recruiter. He has a very direct manner and works with a very specific kind of company, and he's very successful at it.

Each of these recruiters is different, just like every company is different. Finding the right recruiter can lead to a long-term relationship in which the recruiter is able to identify exactly the kind of person your company wants.

It sounds funny to say but recruiters are like snowflakes: no two are the same. That's because it's all about relationships and no two people are the same. One recruiter may work better with some companies than others. Some may know a particular industry better than others. The important thing is to find one that you identify with, who understands your company and your unique needs and objectives.

The business of recruiting

There are several types of business arrangements when working with a recruiter.

In a **retained agreement** the company makes periodic payments to the recruiter for an in-place recruiting plan, regardless of whether a candidate is hired or not since the ultimate decision to hire is beyond the recruiter's control. The idea is that the recruiter will deliver quality, worthy candidates as the goal of this arrangement. This is accepted practice for management recruiting.

An additional consideration involved in a retained agreement is that the recruiter takes a much more thorough, attentive approach. The supporting documentation that backs the hiring decision and the competitive information gathered during the search can become as important as the subsequent list of candidate finalists. In addition to being valuable to management, this data may be used for reporting to state or federal oversight agencies.

A **contingency agreement** is based on a defined outcome, such as the hire, and payment is made once the outcome is achieved. With no up-front financial commitment from the client, the client assumes less financial risk and the recruiter is not committed to a time-consuming, detailed search. Contingency agreements can be useful for lower to mid-level management recruiting. However the relationship between client and recruiter may be more uncertain as the recruiter is free to concentrate on retained agreements or other ventures.

A **container fee agreement** blends the *contingency* and *retainer* agreements. It includes an initial payment required for the planning and execution of services, with the balance tied to the hire itself. Thus the final payment would be contingent on the hire taking place, creating a more equitable share of risk and reward for both the recruiter and client.

Many recruiters offer various levels of service to accommodate clients' needs. Fee structures are based on the agreed-upon services. For example, while full-project recruiting includes everything from job description through offer, a client may opt to choose candidate screening services only.

Again, recruiting is a people-oriented business. Like any business built on relationships, you may find a range of differences in service and professionalism.

Having a strong recruiter working for you can provide a substantial return on your investment. A recruiter's objectivity puts him in a unique position to serve your best interests. However, just as you need to find the right fit for your open position, you need to find a recruiter who is the right fit for your company. Take the time to evaluate and find a recruiter who will work with you as a trusted, collaborative partner.

Conclusion

In the book, *The Seven Habits of Highly Effective People* by Dr. Stephen R. Covey, he was asked if he had it to do over again, which one thing he would do differently as a businessperson. The answer:

> "I would do more strategic, proactive recruiting and selecting. When you are buried by the urgent and have a thousand balls in the air, it is so easy to put people that appear to have solutions into key positions. The tendency is to not look deeply into their backgrounds and patterns, to do 'due diligence,' nor is it to carefully develop the criteria that needs to be met in the particular roles or assignments. I am convinced that when recruiting and selecting is done strategically, that is, thinking long-term and proactively, not based upon the pressures of the moment, it pays enormous long-term dividends...I am convinced that although training and development is important, recruiting and selection are much more important."[3]

Yet as we have explored in this book, finding the right person for the position requires an intricate, complex process. Expertise in that process could make a huge difference in your bottom line.

A bad hire can cost the company two to five times the individual's salary when you take into account recruiting, training time, and any mistakes on the job. In some cases, a bad hire can have more than a negative financial impact when you add the loss of other employees' morale, management credibility or the company's reputation.

---

[3] *The Seven Habits of Highly Effective People*, Dr. Stephen R. Covey, Simon & Schuster 1989, page 329

At the same time, the passive candidate pool is bigger than ever. According to Donna Weiss in *Talent Magazine*, nearly 50 percent of the labor pool falls into the passive category, that is, those not searching for employment. "That said, active candidates — many of whom are unemployed or underemployed — are working hard to get recruiters' attention. The average number of applications a recruiter receives for a given job posting increased by 167 percent from 2007 to 2011 according to CEB's annual 'Candidate Rules of Engagement' study."[4] The same study found that just 35 percent of applicants meet the basic job requirements in a typical search.

This and the present economy, which leaves many hesitant to make a move, complicate an already complex process of finding the right person for your position. It requires a great deal of time, creativity, and an understanding of emerging trends and technologies. It mandates smarter sourcing: extending your reach beyond the active labor pool through social media, technology and networking.

The level of difficulty involved in finding the right fit for your position also suggests the need to look inward. Align your corporate goals throughout your organization. Communicate your objectives effectively to your employees. Demonstrate the value you place on your employees and look to them for insight into what is working and what needs work.

A good hire is a win-win situation for everyone. A bad hire is not just a matter of inconvenience; it can generate financial, administrative and legal complications and even impact your company's reputation. Take the time to find, attract and hire the right people.

Success in a company is a combination of finding the right people and having them in the right place. This must be executed with a good corporate structure with ample support.

<u>Great companie</u>s – those that outperform the competition – do

[4] http://talentmgt.com/articles/view/avoid-post-and-pray-recruiting

not have to have phenomenal infrastructure, significant cash flow or even a great product or service. Great companies have the ability to hire and retain good employees. They are able to recruit for bench depth and attract the right people.

Whether you're recruiting for your own company or working with a recruiter, think of the word *recruit* this way:

R ealistic

E lastic

C oncern

R educe

U nited

I nitiative

T imely

You must be *realistic* in your expectations and deadlines. There are no perfect candidates – or perfect companies -- and you must be realistic in your goal setting and understanding of industry and market prospects.

You must be *elastic*, or flexible, in both your expectations and time lines. Every candidate is not going to have 100% of what you have on your wish list. Be prepared to pick and choose what is most important to your goals. Be prepared to take the time with a thorough recruiting process.

Your hiring authority must have *concern* for and empathy with the individual in question. He must have the ability to develop the relationship with a cautious individual into one of trust.

You need the ability to *reduce* the time the hiring process takes and simplify the complexities of the process as much as possible.

Again, this is most often accomplished with an outside recruiter who is an expert in the field.

You must be *united,* whether working with a recruiter in partnership to achieve your objectives or various members and levels of your own team. This requires open communication, sharing of information and a united understanding of the value of the position and company objectives.

A recruiting authority must be able to *initiate*, that is, be *proactive* and not *reactive*. This is a key step in the recruiting process and helps reduce the overall length of time of the processes. I personally believe it is critical to be proactive and take the time for fire drills along the way so that when there is a fire, you are ready. Reacting usually gives rise to unnecessary costs and delays.

Finally, the recruiting process must be *timely* to fill your gap as quickly and productively as possible. The hiring authority must keep things in motion, improving the flow of the process so that it is never stilted. He must ensure that everyone knows his role and everything moves along at a suitable and constructive pace.

Success in recruiting is not a matter of luck. It requires an acute understanding of human nature, a keen awareness of the markets and candidates, plenty of preparation and hard work. It is driven by an idea of where to head, a vision.

Once you've hired the right people, it's important to keep them. Engage them, motivate them, support them, recognize and reward them. Invest in the right people – your people – and your company will see a huge return.

You've heard that a chain is only as strong as its weakest link. A great company is only as strong as its weakest hire. Work to build your team, from the very beginning when you're developing your job description, through the hiring and onboarding processes, and beyond to long-term retention.

Recognize that your people are your greatest asset. Use your recruiting process to strengthen that asset and the power of proactive recruiting will turn a good company into a great company. It will improve your bottom line, your industry presence and augment your corporate growth. Proactive recruiting will set a solid foundation that will take you to a flourishing future, even despite a contrary economy.

Acknowledgements

This book has changed more than 100 times over the last three years. Throughout the grinding research, edits, and rewrites, there have been many people who assisted me in completing this book. During the last 30 years, I have been privileged to work with, be mentored by, and be educated on the topics of this book by so many formidable people. From college professors, fellow graduate school students, managers, supervisors, mentors, fellow professionals in the staffing and recruiting industry, and clients who have engaged me to help solve recruiting dilemmas, I have been fortunate to encounter and learn from so many.

I wrote this book in summary form so that it could be used as a reference guide in a pinch or a good read that would not take a long time to get through. I am thankful to many people for their insight, guidance, advice, feedback, and stories that helped craft the message and lessons on recruiting, staffing, hiring, on-boarding, and retaining your employees.

I first would like to thank you, the reader. You chose to read on this topic so it must be important to you.

I wrote this book to provide a venue to enrich the recruiting practices through my ideas and explain the importance of the major topics explored here. It is my hope that through education, the readers of this book will be more effective and successful managers, business owners, or hiring authorities. It is my hope that you, the reader, will be able to grasp the sometimes complex issues on key topics and come away with some solid, applicable ideas. My contact information is provided at the end for you to call me and discuss the information presented here.

From my years in the higher education at Richard Stockton College and Temple University, I would like to thank Dr. Charles P. Hall for his focus on detail in reading and research. Thank you to Neilson "Pa" Wood, whose high standard of writing prose made me always triple check my work. Thank you to James Bausman and William Sites, who showed me to listen to your gut but know that the "truth is in the verification" and that is where you put your money. Thank you to Christopher Connors, Kevin Erdman, and James Cavagnaro who have served as examples that with the right people on the bus, a company has a fighting chance to succeed.

Thanks to Allan Atzrott who taught me the importance of working through issues to overcome adversity.

Thanks to Greg Hare for his assistance on the chapter on legal perspectives.

Thanks to Marilyn Jackson for her support in mentoring me in recruiting. She taught me that recruiting is a profession not a job. She is like my third mother and my primary business advisor.

To four professionals from NAPS have helped me develop an outline for the basis of the book and a recruiting career Robert P. Style, Esq., Dr. Frank Burnett, Tony and Barbara Bruno.

To Stu Goldblatt, Jeff Traill, and Al Meyer: Thanks for being great recruiters who I have enjoyed working with for many years.

Thanks to Karen and Phil Holt, who recruited me in my first two sales jobs and took a chance by hiring me as a recruiter at Sales Recruiters, Inc. I have enjoyed being connected with the company since 1995.

Special thanks to Robyn Sweeney for her advice on her 30 years' of people management, and as my wife for unconditional support of my efforts to write this book, and to Hunter and Xiara, my children, for giving up time with me so I could work on and complete my book.

Thanks to Bob Sweeney, my father-in-law, for providing the vision: "It does not get any better than this." I am deeply indebted to him for the guidance, support and encouragement he gave me before he passed away.

To my brother John Verity, thanks for teaching me the importance of "Seeking first to understand, then to be understood," and being my first role model.

Thank you to Shirley Nocitra for teaching me the key aspects involved in running a small business.

Thanks to my father, Dr. Joseph Glickel, for providing me a good work and professional role model. He did not realize it before his passing but he helped me craft my mantra that I live by today: "Achieve, Succeed, Aspire, and Inspire."

To Kirk Wilson for his help on the book formatting for the print version. Also thank you to Ellie Bickert Augsburger for her work on the book cover.

To Linda Metzger, Vice President of Human Resources and Administration at BAO, I am grateful. She could plow through my ideas both written and spoken to find the nugget of usable recruiting program additions. Also, the Higgins family, the management, the recruiting and training departments as well as the employees of BAO (By Appointment Only), who provided me a laboratory to define, test, and refine my thoughts and programs: Thank you. Of all the companies I have ever worked with, worked for, recruited for, or consulted to, BAO is my most memorable experience because of the people in all levels of responsibility throughout the company. I do not know if I will ever see a place where recruiting and people are held in such high regard. To Victoria Wilson and Ellen Keith for proofreading and helping me edit drafts.

I would like to thank Susan Boerchers, my friend who helped me to take my ideas and transcribe and rework them until others could understand what I was trying to say. She can take words and make them convey my real thoughts. It is a talent that I respect and admire.

John Sacerdote, the former president of the National Association of Personnel Services who wrote the forward to this book, thank you. When I requested that he write the foreword for this book, he agreed without hesitation.

Writing this book has been an enjoyable exercise and professionally enriching experience. Apart from people and parties aforementioned, there are many others who contributed. I apologize that I could not give everyone the recognition due to the lack of space. Many have contributed to my education and appreciation of the complex systems, beliefs, and practices of recruiting, staffing, and on-boarding. I appreciate their assistance and thank them for their advice and support.

Thanks to all!

Henry Glickel, CPC, CERS
Recruitment and Retention Search Executive
Cell: 603-770-7175
http://www.henryglickel.com/

About the author

Henry J. Glickel, CPC, CERS, has nearly 20 years of experience in recruiting, during which time he has successfully completed more than 1,000 searches for hundreds of companies in the areas of sales, accounting/finance, IT, human resources, client services, management, executives and members of the C-suite and Board of Directors for private companies of various sizes.

He has been associated with Sales Recruiters, Inc. (www.sales-recruiters.com) since 1995, having served as recruiter, manager, president, and consultant. Henry became a consultant to Barclay Personnel Systems (www.barclaypersonnel.com) in January 2011 when Barclay and Sales Recruiters merged their services to create a new synergy to meet the growing needs of its client base. In addition to his continued role at SRI/Barclay, he is currently manager of talent acquisition and employee retention for By Appointment Only, Inc. (BAO) (www.baoinc.com). Henry was named "Most Valuable Player" by the president of BAO, Inc. in 2006.

Henry holds the National Association of Personnel Services' (NAPS) (www.recruitinglife.com) Certified Placement Consultant (CPC) and Certified Employee Retention Specialist (CERS) designations. The CERS credential, along with the prerequisite CPC or he Certified Temporary Staffing Specialist (CTS), are the only national designations recognized globally by the personnel Services and staffing industry. At the time of the CERS designation, Henry was one of only 40 professionals to hold the designation. In 2013, Henry was selected to conduct the training and proctoring of the CERS coursework and examination for NAPS.

Henry serves on the Northern New England Association of Personnel Services Board of Directors and is active in his local community through the Chamber of Commerce, New England Association of Personnel Services, and in the past, Big Brothers/Big Sisters of Greater Lawrence and Southern New Hampshire. Henry was also involved with Junior Achievement of Philadelphia and Family Promise of Greater Rockingham County of NH.

An acknowledged leader in the industry, Henry has been published numerous times in *Sales and Marketing Executive Report*, *Selling Magazine's Special Report*, *Selling Power*, *Fortune Small Business*, *Metrowest Daily News*, *Selling Crossing Magazine, and Outsourcing Center*.

He holds a Bachelor's Degree with Magna Cum Laude honors from Richard Stockton College in Pomona, NJ, and an MBA in Health Administration with honors from Temple University in Philadelphia, PA. He is married and lives in Salem, NH with his wife and two children.

www.ingramcontent.com/pod-product-compliance
Lightning Source LLC
Chambersburg PA
CBHW060859170526
45158CB00001B/425